the
Hershberg
Diet

the Hershberg Diet

Lose weight quickly, comfortably
and for life

Dr Melissa Hershberg

metro

Published by Metro, an imprint of
John Blake Publishing Ltd,
3 Bramber Court, 2 Bramber Road,
London W14 9PB, England

www.blake.co.uk

First published in Canada by Key Porter Books Limited, Toronto, Canada 2007
First published in paperback in the UK in 2008

ISBN 978 1 84454 496 7

British Library Cataloguing-in-Publication Data:

A catalogue record for this book is available from the British Library.

Design by www.envydesign.co.uk

Printed and bound in Great Britain by William Clowes Ltd, Beccles, Suffolk

1 3 5 7 9 10 8 6 4 2

Papers used by John Blake Publishing are natural, recyclable products made from wood grown
in sustainable forests. The manufacturing processes conform to the environmental regulations
of the country of origin.

Every attempt has been made to contact the relevant copyright-holders, but some were unobtainable.
We would be grateful if the appropriate people could contact us.

CONTENTS

*This book is dedicated to all people who have ever
struggled with their weight*

*There is no such thing as a bad body, just bad clothing,
bad mirrors and bad diets*

MELISSA HERSHBERG

Introducing
The Hershberg Diet

What If?

We all know how to lose weight; it's simple, right? We just have to avoid eating carbs, fat and sugar.

Wait a minute, what about fibre? That's a carb and it's good for weight loss, isn't it? What about the fat content? Should we eat only good fats or avoid fat altogether? What's the glycaemic index (GI)? Should we use the GI to guide us and, if so, why isn't the GI value listed on the foods we buy? Some of us think the trick to losing weight is high-protein foods. Some people avoid fat, while others indulge in it so long as the carbohydrate content is low. Some of us read nutrition labels, others don't.

As you can see, despite our years of obsessing over our eating and weight, we don't have a universal and systematic process to use when approaching eating – and it shows. Despite our fixation on weight and the countless fad diets occupying bookstore shelves, approximately one billion people worldwide are considered to be dangerously overweight. According to a Health Survey for England undertaken in 2005 (links to it can be found at www.ic.nhs.uk/ statistics-and-data-collections/health-and-lifestyles/obesity), it is estimated that 21.2 per cent of English men and 21.5 per cent of women can be classified as obese; 16.8 per cent of boys and 16.9 per cent of girls aged 2-10 in England were classified obese. Even more alarmingly, the numbers are projected to increase unless we put a stop to all this confusion. But wait...

What if I revealed that there was a system to correct this problem – a revolutionary weight-loss system that could teach anyone to lose weight and improve their health in just under an hour or two?

What if I told you that the system was based on a unique, never-before revealed combination of three breakthrough nutritional concepts, and so long as you understood these three concepts, you could lose weight easily, quickly and permanently? Even better, you could lose weight while eating *any* food that you like: fat, carbs, you name it. You could even eat fatty carbs and the weight would still come off. No hunger, no deprivation required.

What if I told you that the system was centred around the discovery of a secret 'fourth macronutrient' and that this 'fourth macronutrient' is the key to understanding eating for both health and weight loss? Even better, what if I promised that I could prove it to you?

Finally, what if I told you that the system is so easy to implement that it requires no counting grams of fat, protein or carbohydrates? Would you be intrigued?

Introducing a doctor-designed, breakthrough approach to healthy eating and weight loss – The Hershberg Diet!

The Problem

Before you go on to learn the Hershberg Diet system, I'd like to discuss a growing problem – one more serious than obesity – that has become so prevalent in recent years that medical professionals across the globe now consider it a full-blown epidemic. It is currently estimated that 1 in 4 North Americans suffers from this problem; UK research suggests a similar number of people are affected here. It plagues men and women, adults and children around the world, as well as the doctors desperate to treat it. So what is it?

The problem is a new medical phenomenon, a type of syndrome that has surfaced in recent years as a direct result of the improper eating habits that have permeated our world. Some call it Syndrome X; others refer to it as the Metabolic Syndrome. I refer to it as, simply, 'the Syndrome'. Its presence is undeniable; it affects 25 per cent of us!

Even if you have not yet heard of the Syndrome, you will. In fact, a large majority of you are already at risk. For instance:

1. Do you have high blood pressure?
2. Do you tend to gain weight around your mid-section?
3. Do you seem to constantly struggle with your weight despite eating less than others?
4. Do you suffer from gout?
5. Do you often find yourself wandering back to the fridge or biscuit tin within only an hour or so of a satisfying meal?
6. Do you suffer from high cholesterol?
7. Are you an adult woman who still struggles with acne, unwanted facial and body hair and irregular periods?
8. Do you have family members with diabetes?
9. Has your doctor told you that your blood sugar is too high?
10. Do you often skip breakfast, eat a small lunch and then binge in the evenings?

11. Do you ever feel so hungry that you start to feel sweaty or shaky, and have trouble thinking or concentrating?
12. Do you ever feel high from eating, so much so that you often want to keep eating despite feeling full?

If you answered yes to any of the above questions, you are probably at risk for the Syndrome. In fact, if you answered yes to four of the questions (see below), you may already have the Syndrome.

While not a disease, the Syndrome represents a clustering of risk factors for heart disease, stroke and cancer. In essence, having the Syndrome means that you have a cluster of disorders related to your metabolism, all occurring at the same time. These disorders include:

- obesity, particularly around the abdomen (i.e., an 'apple shape')
- high blood pressure
- abnormal cholesterol (i.e., an elevated level of a blood fat known as triglycerides and a decreased level of the good cholesterol known as HDL)
- insulin resistance (i.e., elevated blood sugar levels).

Having one of the above disorders increases your likelihood of the others; the more components of the Syndrome you have, the greater your risk for heart attack, stroke, diabetes and certain forms of cancer. Because these afflictions develop in unison, most people who originally see their doctor for high blood pressure find out that they also have high cholesterol and are then watched closely for the development of diabetes (high blood sugar). This is how patients progress quickly from being on no medication and requiring relatively few doctor visits to all of a sudden needing to take four daily medications, with the resulting check-ups, pill changes and side effect management and treatment. It's the Syndrome. It's a drug company's dream, a doctor's nightmare. And by and large a patient's choice.

You see, unlike other ailments and diseases, the Syndrome is fair. It does not happen by chance, nor does it happen overnight. It happens slowly and predictably with warnings along the way. It offers us a chance to avoid it, reverse it, and beat it. Even better, it offers us a chance to do so drug-free. But we don't.

Study after study has revealed to physicians that the underlying cause of the Syndrome is obesity and improper eating habits. Doctors have known about this diet–health connection for years. After all, it makes sense. Eat too much fat, you'll end up with chronically high levels of fat in the blood (triglycerides). Eat too much sugar, you'll end up with chronically high levels of sugar in the blood (diabetes). The medical literature clearly instructs doctors that the first line of treatment for high blood pressure is diet and exercise. The first line of treatment for high cholesterol is diet and exercise. The first line of treatment for diabetes is diet and exercise. And guess what? The first line of treatment for belly fat is diet and exercise! Obviously, the first line of treatment for the Syndrome is diet and exercise! We know the answer! It's being shouted loud and clear. So why aren't we listening? Why are patients still unaware of this link? Why on earth are we allowing a preventable disease to reach epidemic proportions? More importantly, why have most people still not even heard of the Syndrome?

Some may point to the drug companies. The world's top-grossing drugs treat the components of the Syndrome, so the pharmaceutical companies thrive because of the Syndrome. Most individuals with the Syndrome take at least four medications per day and most often do so for life. Moreover, the pills often cause side effects, which are treated with – you guessed it – more pills.

Encouraging diet and exercise is simply bad for business; they work and they're cheap. But the drug companies suffer.

Perhaps it has nothing to do with the drug companies. Maybe the dreaded D&E (diet and exercise) conjures up such thoughts of deprivation, starvation, exhaustion and misery that people just don't think the sacrifice is worth it. For example, I have heard patients say that living a few years longer is simply not worth giving up the foods they love. I've been told it's about quality of life as opposed to quantity.

And I couldn't agree more. But does life with the Syndrome really allow for higher-quality living that is worth sacrificing longevity? Let's consider what life with the Syndrome is like.

While the Syndrome encompasses a cluster of risk factors for heart attack and stroke, these aren't necessarily how sufferers will die. Remember, the Syndrome attacks slowly, gradually and progressively. In other words, the Syndrome operates by slowly eating away at the quality of your life. Consider some of the following afflictions that affect people with the Syndrome.

Chronic Kidney Failure

It is estimated that there are roughly one million people worldwide who require dialysis for chronic renal failure (http://bmj.bmjjournals.com/cgi/content/full/327/7413/463). Being on dialysis means spending up to 12 hours per week in the hospital hooked up to a machine – often for the rest of your life. This certainly would reduce quality of life, as frequent symptoms include nausea, fatigue and loss of appetite. Furthermore, with such a demanding yet necessarily strict schedule, freedom is limited and travel is often no longer possible.

The leading causes of kidney failure are diabetes and high blood pressure.

Limb Amputations

Elevated blood pressure and blood sugar (diabetes) damages blood vessels and nerves. This makes it extremely difficult for the body to heal wounds, even with the help of antibiotics. Often, the only solution to stop the spread of damage is amputation.

According to recent research, people with diabetes are 15 times more at risk of lower limb amputation than people without the condition. Even more alarming, data published by Diabetes UK in 2006 (www.diabetes.org.uk/About_us/News_Landing_Page/2678/) showed that up to 70 per cent of people die within five years of having an amputation.

Impotence

Impotence is the inability to obtain or maintain an erection. Although rarely spoken about, impotence is very common among men with the Syndrome. In impotence caused by high blood sugar (diabetes), the nerves that cause an erection may be damaged. In impotence caused by high blood pressure and high cholesterol, the penile artery may be blocked. Impotence can also be the result of medications used to treat high blood pressure. Oh, and by the way, if you have heart disease that requires that you use nitroglycerin to treat angina, as many people with the Syndrome do, Viagra is contraindicated (no longer a safe option). Sorry.

Arthritis

Arthritis, or joint pain, significantly decreases the quality of life of many individuals. It is one of the most common reasons for an elderly individual to visit the doctor. While arthritis results from years of wear and tear on the joints of the hips, knees and back, for example, the affliction is often experienced earlier and to a more severe degree in individuals with the Syndrome. Why? Well, put simply, years of being overweight translates into years of forcing our joints to sustain that extra weight. This leads to irreversible joint damage for which, unfortunately, aside from total joint replacement, there is often no good treatment or cure.

Cancer

Obese people are more likely to be inactive and eat poor diets, both of which can independently increase their cancer risk. Experts think that about a quarter of all cancer deaths are caused by unhealthy diets and obesity. A report from the American Cancer Society reported in *The New England Journal of Medicine*, April 24, 2003, found that the higher the body mass index (weight divided by height squared), the greater the risk of cancer. Among the heaviest participants, the risk of death from cancer was 52 per cent higher in men and 62 per cent higher in women compared to people of normal weight. Moreover, the data showed that the heaviest men were more likely to die from stomach or prostate cancer, while cancer of the breast, uterus, cervix or ovary were most likely to cause death among the heaviest women.

The study also indicated that excess weight in the abdomen region (as occurs with the Syndrome) can increase the risk of cancer and that people with obesity may be more likely to develop painful gallstones and acid reflux disease – which can also lead to certain cancers.

Quality of Life

So the 'quality of life' argument does not make sense.

The most likely reason that doctors across the globe watch countless patients, young and old, succumb to the Syndrome despite being fully aware of its cause and consequences is because *diet is difficult to prescribe*. While doctors are trained to choose between the countless blood pressure pills, cholesterol pills and diabetes pills on the market, they are provided with relatively little knowledge on how to choose between the countless diets currently available. For instance, it is unclear whether to counsel patients to eat low-carb or low-fat foods. It is unclear whether to counsel patients about calorie counting and portion control or to simply focus all efforts on teaching about the quality of foods being consumed. The latest literature talks about the glycaemic index, but it is time-consuming to rate the glycaemic index of individual foods, let alone meals, and, for the most part, most doctors have no idea how to do this. Doctors need a method that is inexpensive and easy to teach, yet offers a prescription that is sensible, easy and enjoyable for patients and – best of all – will work for life. As you'll soon see, this is the Hershberg Diet.

One of the reasons I entered medicine was to help patients by way of prevention. The practice of medicine was supposed to have shifted in recent years. No longer is it solely about the treatment of symptoms and disease, it's now about health promotion and disease prevention. It's about stopping diseases before they start, as opposed to focusing on treating them once they've already developed. Or so I thought. Yet I found myself watching patient after patient succumb to the Syndrome: a preventable disease! I found myself frustrated and cynical – and I had only just begun. And so I found myself motivated to engender a change. Moreover, I knew that I had the means to do so.

You see, at the age of 15, I virtually stopped eating. My life up until that point had revolved around competitive gymnastics. With a rigorous training schedule of 20+ hours in the gym per week, weight control was never really much of a concern for me. However, when an acute injury abruptly ended my gymnastics career, I found myself gaining weight quickly and unexpectedly. And so I stopped eating. Sure I lost weight – too much weight in fact – but I was miserable and unhealthy. So I began to educate myself about food and nutrition. It was at this point, over 10 years ago, that I discovered what is now the Hershberg Diet system. While I didn't have the scientific or medical knowledge to explain it back then, I knew that it worked, and would work for life. I just didn't know why.

After a science degree and a medical degree, I am happy to report that I now know why. As you will learn in Chapter 1, the explanation rests on the discovery of the 'fourth macronutrient'. Once I was able to identify this 'fourth macronutrient', I was instantly able to articulate and prove the efficacy of the system that I have sworn by for years. I knew that I had discovered a system that could help millions of people lose weight and beat the Syndrome. What I didn't know was how I would convince others that I had the solution. After all, you can imagine the scepticism I encountered – a recent graduate proclaiming to have an innovative diet plan suitable for treating the medical epidemic of the 21st century! Who on earth would believe that?

Well, after being questioned and ridiculed, I was able to convince friends, family, patients and colleagues. Why? Because the system works – and science and math prove it.

I promise that there is no other dietary system that makes more sense and is easier to understand or follow. This system not only helps you shed weight quickly but also provides a lifelong strategy that will help you maintain your weight and beat the Syndrome.

Overview

I have divided the book into two parts: Part One, The Science, and Part Two, The Hershberg Diet Weight-Loss Plan. In Part One, I introduce and explain three breakthrough nutritional concepts. In Part Two, I'll give you a structured and easy-to-follow four-phase diet plan. It's that simple.

PART ONE: The Science

In Part One, you'll find out about the three breakthrough nutritional concepts that form the basis of the Hershberg Diet. Let's have a peek at them now.

1. **The 'fourth macronutrient'** The first and most important concept is how to recognize the 'fourth macronutrient'. In addition to the three macronutrients with which you may be familiar (fat, protein and carbohydrate), there is a 'fourth macronutrient' to consider. This overlooked and ignored 'fourth macronutrient', revealed in Chapter 1, is the key to understanding weight loss. The higher a food is in this 'fourth macronutrient'. the better it is for weight loss. Once you understand how to identify and factor in this 'fourth macronutrient', you will never look at foods, or nutrition labels, in the same way. To lose weight comfortably and quickly, you must learn how to determine which foods are highest in the 'fourth macronutrient'. These are the foods best for weight loss. As you will see in Chapter 1, this is a mathematical fact and I can prove it!

2. **The 'hotty' effect** The second important concept is 'hotty' foods. These foods are so named because eating them

encourages the body to heat up and burn calories. 'Hotty' foods are difficult for the body to digest and metabolise and, as a result, calories are burned – the body literally heats up as a result. Furthermore, many 'hotty' foods and drinks activate hormones that can encourage weight loss. Imagine that! Eating can actually help us lose weight – now, that's hot!

3. **The hormonal effect** The third and final concept that you will learn is how to avoid insulin resistance. In addition to helping prevent cardiovascular disease and diabetes, this knowledge will help you understand why you may be gaining weight despite eating very little. The explanation almost always resides in the body's response to insulin, a hormone released from the pancreas that encourages the storage of fat when handled incorrectly. You will learn that when you overconsume or improperly combine foods that spike blood sugar and insulin, you create a hormonal situation that encourages the body to store fat. You will learn how to train your body to better handle insulin to create a hormonal environment more suited for weight loss.

PART TWO: The Hershberg Diet Weight-Loss Plan

The Hershberg Diet weight-loss plan is divided into four easy phases:

PHASE One Phase One is a two-week initiation phase. It is the strictest phase of the diet. Foods high in the 'fourth macronutrient' are emphasized. By the end of this phase, you will notice a significant change in your body: unhealthy high-sugar cravings will be reduced and your body will already begin to look and feel better as fat tissue is lost and water retention decreases.

PHASE Two The next two weeks will constitute Phase Two of the diet plan. This phase is less strict, as you can now include foods that are lower in the 'fourth macronutrient'. However, these foods still possess the proper 'hotty' and hormonal effect, so weight loss will continue as metabolism and fat-burning hormones remain elevated.

PHASE Three Phase Three is the final phase for weight loss. You will remain in this phase until you reach your goal weight. In this phase, you can eat any food you like, although the majority of your diet will still consist of the foods introduced in Phases One and Two. I will show you how you can afford to treat yourself every day and still lose weight while promoting your health.

PHASE Four Phase Four is maintenance. You will remain in this phase for life! The Hershberg Diet system is not a fad diet; it's a healthy lifestyle.

Additional Content

Throughout Phases One and Two, I will include TIPS boxes to highlight additional benefits associated with the foods that you will be eating. For example, you will learn which foods can help attack menstrual cramps and bloating as well as which foods to eat to help prevent prostate and colon cancer. I will show you how drinking the proper drinks and using certain spices can help you speed weight loss and promote your health.

Phases One and Two also include an extensive collection of recipes that are practical, delicious and easy. For instance, you will learn how to cook the perfect veggie and cheese omelette while brushing your teeth and how to cook a complete dinner of fish and vegetables to perfection in just five minutes. I even provide you with recommended brand names for ready-to-eat shop-bought items. No plan could be simpler. On the Hershberg Diet, not having time to eat well is never an excuse!

Phases One, Two, and Three all contain day-by-day sample menu plans. You may follow the plans exactly or simply use them as guides.

My revolutionary approach to eating will change the way you view food. You will feel neither hungry nor deprived. With the Hershberg Diet weight-loss plan, you can eat any, and as much, food as you like, provided that you use the strategies you learn here in this book.

The Hershberg Diet is an easy-to-follow, sensible, and – most of all – enjoyable eating plan.

Let's get started!

PART ONE

The Science of The Hershberg Diet

CHAPTER 1

The Secret 'Fourth Macronutrient'

TRUE OR FALSE?

Q: Despite our obsession with thinness, diet books and health products, the large majority of us are still completely unaware of the most important and fundamental concept underlying the understanding of nutrition and weight loss.

A: True!

Don't believe me? Consider this:

Almost every medical text, nutritionist and diet that I have come across states that there are three macronutrients (protein, carbohydrate and fat) that constitute all food. You have probably heard this before. If you haven't, consider the diets that have been popular over the decades. They are either low-fat (think Susan Powter in the '90s), low-carbohydrate (think Atkins) or low-protein (think poorly constructed vegan/vegetarian diets). We are a society that has altered our fat, carb and protein ratios for years, yet continues to grow heavier and heavier!

I propose that it is this accepted basic nutritional principle that is responsible for our dietary failures. This flawed principle will continue to hamper even our most valiant weight-loss efforts. Before we can adopt healthy eating habits, lose weight, keep it off and – most importantly – teach our children how to eat, we must recognise that there are **four** macronutrients.

In this chapter, you will learn how to recognize this 'fourth macronutrient' and how to incorporate it into your understanding of food and nutrition labels. As you'll see, it is the single most important factor to consider when deciding how good a food is for weight loss.

Before I open your eyes to this secret 'fourth macronutrient', let's quickly review the other three (protein, carbs and fat), along with some basic nutritional principles. Bear with me while we review the basics; the information that follows will change the way you view food, nutrition labels and weight loss forever!

The Macronutrients

Protein Proteins comprise mostly carbon, hydrogen, oxygen, and nitrogen atoms. These atoms make up amino acids that link together in various ways to create the variety of proteins found within our bodies (i.e., hair, muscle, nails) and foods. Examples of foods high in protein are meats, fish, poultry, and some legumes. **Proteins contain 4 calories per gram.**

Carbohydrates All carbohydrates consist of carbon, hydrogen and oxygen atoms linked together to form sugars. Those that consist of one sugar molecule are called simple sugars and include glucose, fructose and galactose. Those that contain two simple sugars linked together include lactose (milk sugar), sucrose (table sugar) and maltose (malt sugar). Polysaccharides consist of many simple sugars linked together to create starch, cellulose and glycogen. Polysaccharides are big and complex; for that reason starch is often called a complex carbohydrate. Complex carbohydrates don't dissolve in water like the simple sugars, but rather absorb water. Examples of foods high in carbohydrates are breads, pasta, rice, potatoes, desserts (like cake, doughnuts, etc.) and sweets, milk, fruits and some vegetables. **Carbohydrates contain 4 calories per gram.**

Fat Dietary fats consist mainly of carbon and hydrogen atoms. When they are solid at room temperature, they are called fats; when they are liquid, we call them oils. Saturated fats (e.g., in butter, red meat, cream, cheese and egg yolk) tend to be from animal sources. Unsaturated fats, either monosaturated or polyunsaturated (i.e., olive oil, vegetable oil, canola oil, nuts and seeds), tend to be from plant sources. Polyunsaturated fats contain the essential fatty acids, such as omega-6 and omega-3 fatty acids, that we must get from our diet because our bodies cannot make them. Good sources of omega-6 are unrefined corn, sesame and sunflower oils. Good sources of omega-3 are oily fish like salmon, flaxseed oil, pumpkin seeds, walnuts and dark green vegetables. The third type of fat is trans fat, sometimes called hydrogenated fat, which is usually man-made and found in fatty snack foods like chips and biscuits. While unsaturated fats can be good for us, hydrogenated and saturated fats, if overeaten, are associated with an increased risk of heart and blood vessel disease. **Fats contain 9 calories per gram.**

Calories

Dieting trends over the last few decades have avoided acknowledging calories at all costs. The '90s catchphrase 'Calories don't make you fat, fat makes you fat' exemplifies the lunacy of this concept. Calories are nothing more than units of energy; they tell us how much a food is worth in terms of energy content. So when we say that a chocolate bar has 300 calories, we are saying that, after digestion and metabolism, our bodies can potentially receive 300 calories worth of energy from that chocolate bar.

What happens if the body doesn't need that energy though? If we consume more calories than we burn off, we will gain weight. This is not a new concept, nor is it refutable. Remember learning about Newton in high school? His first law of thermodynamics says that energy is neither created nor destroyed, it just changes forms. Well, when it comes to nutrition, the energy (calories) contained in a food, if not spent to fuel our bodies, will get stored as fat for later use. If we keep consuming more energy than we need, our fat stores will certainly add up!

Before we go on to see how all of this information comes together on a nutrition label, let's quickly review the main points:

- Fat contains 9 calories of energy per gram.
- Proteins and carbohydrates each contain 4 calories of energy per gram.
- Calories are units of energy.
- If we consume more calories from food than our body burns off, we will gain weight.

Nutrition Labels and the Secret 'Fourth Macronutrient'

Let's take a quick example that explains why we need to understand nutrition labels: fat-free turkey from the deli.

(Before I begin, please note that this example, plus the two that I will present in a few moments, may give some life-long avoiders of maths a bit of a headache! To prove my point that we absolutely must recognize the 'fourth macronutrient' if we want to understand weight loss once and for all, I must take you through the mathematical challenges that follow. For many people, this section will be worth the couple of minutes of brainpower required, as it is enlightening. If, however, you choose to just skim it, don't worry. You will not have to do these calculations on the Hershberg Diet weight-loss plan. In fact, I promise you there is no counting of fat grams, carb grams or protein grams required at all!)

Okay, back to our example. Would you agree that turkey is a protein? Yes. Would you agree that 100 grams (3 to 4 ounces) of fat-free turkey is a reasonable portion size? Yes again. Remember, protein costs 4 calories per gram. So, if we do our calculations, one portion of fat-free turkey should cost 100 grams × 4 calories/gram = 400 calories! Wow, that's a lot of calories; after all, a chocolate bar is only about 300 or so calories. What's going on? How can fat-free turkey, a prototypical diet food, cost more calories than a chocolate bar? The answer is that it doesn't; 100 grams of fat-free turkey provides 100 or so calories. What happened? We better take a closer look at nutrition labels to help us sort out the confusion.

Nutrition labels list a food's serving size as well as its calories, fat, protein and carbohydrate content. In addition, there's usually a breakdown (in grams) of the different types of carbohydrates found in the food, such as fibre, sugar and starch. The sodium and salt content is also listed, and as well as the total fat conent, the amount of saturated fats is always listed. All of this adds up to one confusing label!

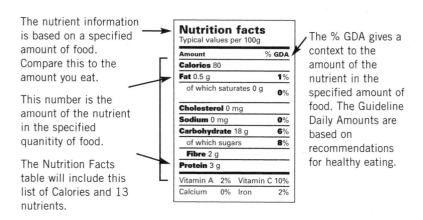

The nutrient information is based on a specified amount of food. Compare this to the amount you eat.

This number is the amount of the nutrient in the specified quanitity of food.

The Nutrition Facts table will include this list of Calories and 13 nutrients.

Nutrition facts
Typical values per 100g

Amount	% GDA
Calories 80	
Fat 0.5 g	1%
of which saturates 0 g	0%
Cholesterol 0 mg	
Sodium 0 mg	0%
Carbohydrate 18 g	6%
of which sugars	8%
Fibre 2 g	
Protein 3 g	

Vitamin A	2%	Vitamin C	10%
Calcium	0%	Iron	2%

The % GDA gives a context to the amount of the nutrient in the specified amount of food. The Guideline Daily Amounts are based on recommendations for healthy eating.

The popular fad diets suggest that so much nutritional data is too much information for consumers to comprehend, so they encourage us to focus only on certain parts of a product's nutrition label. Low-fat diets claim that we need pay attention only to the fat grams, low-carbohydrate diets encourage us to look at the carbohydrate content, and cardiologists tell us to pay particular attention to the amount of saturated fat. Clearly, as people are becoming heavier and heavier, this simplified approach is not working.

We must understand the composition of the food that we are eating and look at the entire label. More importantly, we need to recognise that it is what is **not** on the label that matters the most! Let's look at some more examples, keeping in mind that all carbohydrates are 4 calories per gram, all proteins are 4 calories per gram, and all fats are 9 calories per gram. As you'll see, the factor that we should be paying most attention to, the 'fourth macronutrient', is not included on the nutrition label at all!

Examples

ROMAINE LETTUCE
Serving size 85 grams
Calories 20
Carbohydrates 3 grams
Protein 1 gram
Fat 0.5 gram

Analysis
3 grams **carb** + 1 gram **protein** + 0.5
gram **fat** = 4.5 grams total
3 g **carb** × 4 cal/g = 12 calories
1 g **protein** × 4 cal/g = 4 calories
0.5 g **fat** × 9 cal/g = 4.5 calories

Nutrition Facts

Serving Size 6 leaves (85 g)

Amount For Serving		
Calories 20	Calories from Fat 0	
		% Daily Value*
Total Fat 0.5 g		**1%**
Saturated Fat 0 g		**0%**
Trans Fat 0 g		
Cholesterol 0 mg		**0%**
Sodium 0 mg		**0%**
Potassium 140 mg		**4%**
Total Carbohydrate 3 g		**1%**
Dietary Fibre 1 g		**4%**
Sugars 2 g		
Protein 1 g		
Vitamin A 20%	•	Vitamin C 4%
Calcium 2%	•	Iron 2%

*Percent Daily Values are based on a 2,000 calorie diet. Your daily values may be higher or lower depending on your calorie needs.

	Calories:	2,000	2,500
Total Fat	Less than	65 g	80 g
Sat. Fat	Less than	20 g	25 g
Cholestrol	Less than	300 mg	300 mg
Sodium	Less than	2,400 mg	2,400 mg
Potassium		3,500 mg	3,500 mg
Total Carbohydrates		300 g	375 g
Dietary Fibre		25 g	30 g

Calories per gram:
Fat 9 • Carbohydrates 4 • Protein 4

12 carbohydrate calories +
4 protein calories + 4.5 fat calories = 20.5 calories
3 grams carb + 1 gram protein + 0.5 gram fat = 4.5 grams total
per serving

The calories add up almost perfectly. A serving claims to have 20 calories and we have accounted for 20 calories. The grams don't add up at all though. A serving claims to have 85 grams, but we've only accounted for 4.5 grams. What is the nutrition label not telling us?

Let's take another example.

TUNA: GOLDSEAL® SMOKED LIGHT TUNA INFORMATION

(http://www.goldseal.ca/health/nutrient_tuna.asp)

Serving size 55 grams

Calories 60

Carbohydrates 0 grams

Protein 14 grams

Fat 0.2 grams*

* You may be asking yourself: How is there a half gram of fat in romaine lettuce and only a fifth of a gram in tuna? Remember in the section that described fats, where I mentioned that dark green leafy vegetables (like romaine) are good sources of polyunsaturated fat, specifically omega-3 fatty acids? Well this is explains how tuna and romaine compare in fat content – an interesting comparison indeed.

Nutrition Facts		
Per ¼ cup (55 g)		
Amount		**% Daily Value**
Calories 60		
Fat 0.2 g		1%
Saturated / + Trans /		1%
Cholesterol 30 mg		
Sodium 120 mg		5%
Carbohydrate		0%
Fibre 0 g		0%
Sugars 0 g		
Protein 14 g		
Vitamin A		0%
Vitamin C		0%
Calcium		4%
Iron		2%

Analysis

0 grams **carb** × 4 cal/gram = 0 calories

14 grams **protein** × 4 cal/gram = 56 calories

0.2 gram **fat** × 9 cal/gram = 1.8 calories

0 carbohydrate calories + 56 protein calories + 1.8 fat calories = 57.8 calories

0 grams carb + 14 grams protein + 0.2 gram fat = 14.2 grams total per serving

Again, the calories add up almost perfectly. A serving claims to have 60 calories and we've calculated 57.8 calories. The grams are way off though. A serving claims to have 55 grams but we've only accounted for 14.2 grams. What is the nutrition label not telling us? Where are the missing 40.8 grams of food coming from?

If you haven't figured out why our calculations aren't working, don't feel bad. If we factor in just the three macronutrients (carbohydrates, protein and fat), many nutrition labels will never make sense and consumers will forever be confused.

Now let me enlighten you. Consider a substance that has zero calories per gram. You could add as many grams as you wanted and the calorie count would not change.

Water! Water! Water! Water! Water! Water! Water! Water! Water! Water!

No one ever thinks about the water content of food. This is why people have altered their fat, protein and carbohydrate ratios for years, yet continue to get heavier and heavier! Water is the 'fourth macronutrient' and, as you'll see, it is absolutely imperative that we recognise it as such.

Nutrition labels are becoming more common as companies recognise that consumers are demanding the right to know what is in the food that they are consuming. Yet the constituent that matters most – the 'fourth macronutrient' – is omitted. Now that we understand that water constitutes the 'fourth macronutrient', we can understand why our calculations didn't add up. You see, 100 grams worth of fat-free pre-packed sliced turkey contains only 100 or so calories because it is mostly water. It has roughly 25 grams of protein at 4 calories per gram (25 grams × 4 calories per gram = 100 calories). The other 75 grams of a 100-gram portion must be zero-calorie water. This makes sense. If we consider that romaine lettuce contains 80.5 grams of water at zero calories per gram, we can see how the calories were correct. The same holds true for tuna with 45.8 grams of water. Similarly, grapefruit, which we consider a carbohydrate, should actually be considered a 'water', since the majority of its weight comprises water, hence its low calorie count. If we want to understand weight loss, we must always recognise the 'fourth macronutrient'. We must learn to *eat* water!

When you eat high-water foods, you get full because you are eating a lot in weight (grams). However, you are consuming a very low number of calories; high-water foods have low energy densities and are therefore the best for weight loss. You can eat them often, and in large portions, and still lose weight. In fact, many high-water foods actually encourage your body to burn calories simply from eating them! We will talk more about this in later chapters. For now, simply remember that the higher a food is in water, the more valuable it is for weight loss.

Now that we understand that water is the 'fourth macronutrient', we can start to understand food much better. For instance, why do you think that vegetables 'reduce down' so much when you cook them? They are almost entirely water! As you heat them, whether in the wok, oven or microwave, the water evaporates and you are left with less.

Do an experiment. Take an entire bag of spinach and put it in a empty pot – no water or anything else. Now turn on the heat and stir the spinach a little. What happens? The spinach starts to cook, and although it initially filled the pot, now it doesn't even cover the bottom. Now you can understand why 100 grams of spinach has only about 12 or so calories. It should really be considered a 'water', not a carbohydrate. When we eat foods that are high in water, we get a lot of grams for very few calories. Let's look at how the opposite is true as well.

What do people engaged in high levels of activity, such as a long hike or a canoe trip, like to eat? Trail mix! It's a favourite for providing lots of energy, and is therefore high in calories. Now think about what it contains: dried fruit, granola and nuts. Eating these dry foods allows us to consume loads of calories without getting full. There are no zero-calorie water grams to factor into the amount we are eating. Every bite of that trail mix will be counted as calories. Great for energy, bad for weight loss! Yet many people who don't understand the importance of the 'fourth macronutrient' eat these dried foods and believe that they are good for weight loss. Sorry, but unless you are planning to engage in strenuous physical activity, these dried types of foods can lead to rapid weight gain.

Let's Eat How We Want to Be

It astounds me that our society has ignored water as a macronutrient for so long, considering our biology.

People say that we are what we eat, and I couldn't agree more. When we eat diets that are high in fat and sugar, we tend to become overweight (high body fat) and diabetic (high blood sugar). Our bodies literally turn into fat and sugar! I therefore propose that we eat how we want to be – thin and youthful.

The majority – roughly 60 to 70 per cent – of our body weight is water. Although water makes up the majority of what we are, the percentage varies with age and body fat. The younger and leaner an individual is, the more water she contains, and vice versa. Consider for a moment why pediatricians stress the importance of fluids when a child is sick. Because children need such a high percentage of body water, they cannot afford to lose water like adults can; they dehydrate easily. Often, hydration status determines whether children will be admitted to hospital when sick. Dehydrated children are fatigued and lethargic with sunken eyes and lax skin. They look aged! Water is not only crucial for our biological functioning, but also promotes a youthful, healthy appearance. The more high-water foods we consume, the leaner and younger we will feel and appear.

History has provided obvious hints as well. Before food processing, we ate fresh foods: fruits, vegetables, milk, meats, seeds and grains. However, because of the increasing amounts of high-sugar processed foods like sweets, fizzy drinks, biscuits etc., we no longer satisfy our sweet tooth with healthy fruits. Although both contain sugar, factor in the 'fourth macronutrient'. Sweets and fruits both contain simple sugars as their main ingredient on the nutrition label, but fruit is a high-water, high-fibre food. So we can eat an entire apple for the same calorific price as three or so sweets. Which choice would make you more 'full'? We can consume handfuls of sweets or biscuits at a sitting because there is no water to fill up our stomach. Our stomachs need a critical weight of food to make us feel 'full'. Without the water, our stomachs trigger our brain to tell us to eat larger portions to attain the same fullness – and the calories add up.

If you are still unconvinced, close your eyes and picture a typical convenience store. Picture all the goodies that you would consider buying. I am thinking of crisps, biscuits, chocolate and even supposedly 'healthy' protein bars. Now, notice what all these snack foods have in common. They are dry! They have no free (zero-calorie) water in them. Each time you chew and swallow, you will be consuming calories! Even the protein bars that we think are healthy aren't always! They often have a lot of fat, which is low in water. Fat is hydrophobic, meaning that oil and water don't mix; the fat repels the water. So the more fat a food contains, the less water it will usually contain. Further, fat costs 9 calories per gram; it's pricey! Okay, so what about the high-quality protein contained within these bars, you ask? Well, the protein is in 'isolate' form. This means that the water has been taken out! Now you can understand why protein bars are often marketed as meal replacements. They are so low in water that approximately four bites' worth is equivalent in calorie content to an entire meal. Protein bars are densely packed sources of energy (calories). Again, this is great if you are planning on doing rigorous activity, need a meal replacement, or are trying to put on weight. But if you are not, you will likely be taking in more energy that your body needs. As we have learned, the leftover calories will simply be stored as fat!

It is no coincidence that as our world has become more convenient, our food has become drier, and we have become heavier. We must look back to correct our dietary mistakes.

Chapter Summary

- Water is the 'fourth macronutrient' that is essential to weight loss.
- Water has zero calories per gram.
- The more water a food contains, the better it is for weight loss.

How Fancy Marketing Tricks May Be Making You Fat

Ever heard of low-carb beer or zero-carb rum? I'm sure you have. Almost all alcohol is now marketed as low-carb. Take the advertising for a white rum: zero sugar, zero carbs, 66 calories. Sounds great, doesn't it? Let's put this marketing to the test.

Based on what I've explained so far, there are three basic macronutrients: carbs, protein and fat. However, as we've seen, there really should be four. Water is the fourth macronutrient; it is an essential part of food and contributes to its weight. When we analyze a nutrition label, we must consider how each of the macronutrients is contributing to the food's overall nutritional content. The same theory must be applied to drinks.

If white rum has zero carbs, then where on earth do the 66 calories come from? It isn't protein. It isn't fat – alcohol is fat-free. So where are the calories coming from? If there are no carbs, as the advertisement promises, and no protein nor fat, then it must be the fourth macronutrient, water. But this makes no sense. Water does not get us drunk and, furthermore, water has zero calories.

Stumped? I bet you are. You see, even though I just told you that there are three basic macronutrients, and a fourth, water, that all contribute to the weight of food, there's actually one more. Alcohol itself! Alcohol is a type of macronutrient. It has 7 calories per gram.

To recap:

- Carbohydrates have 4 calories per gram.
- Protein has 4 calories per gram.
- Fat has 9 calories per gram.
- Water has 0 calories per gram.
- Alcohol has 7 calories per gram.

So what exactly is alcohol?

Alcohol is a type of carbohydrate that has been fermented. It contains substances such as fruit, wheat, potato or barley. Wine is made from grapes. Beer is made from barley. Vodka uses wheat or potato. Grapes, barley, wheat and potato are carbs. But for these carbs to turn into alcohol, they must be fermented. After fermentation, the carbohydrate is no longer classified as a carb but rather as an alcohol. So, for instance, when barley is in its natural state, it is a carbohydrate and therefore has 4 calories per gram. However, once it has been fermented, it is considered an alcohol and now contains 7 calories per gram. So alcohol is simply a more calorific type of carbohydrate!

This then raises the question, is low-carb beer actually more calorific than full-carb beer? What do you think?

I'll let you ponder this question for a few moments. Before I answer, though, I'd like to tackle the subject of alcoholic spirits.

Pure alcoholic spirits such as rum, gin, vodka or tequila all have zero carbs because they are distilled.

The distilling process ensures that all of the carbohydrate (e.g., the wheat or potato) has been fermented to alcohol, leaving no carbs behind.

So based on what I've taught, can you guess how many calories 1 ounce of vodka contains?

Well, 1 ounce is equivalent in weight to 28 grams. So if alcohol contains 7 calories per gram and there are zero carbs, zero protein and zero fat, then we may reasonably conclude that 1 ounce (28 grams) of vodka would contain 196 calories, (28 grams × 7 calories per gram = 196).

This seems like a lot doesn't it? Well, of course it does. Remember, vodka isn't 100 per cent alcohol; it's more like 50 per cent alcohol. So this means that the rest, the other 50 per cent, is water. So a 1-ounce (28 gram) serving of vodka contains approximately 14 grams of alcohol (14 grams × 7 calories per gram = 98 calories) and 14 grams of water (14 grams × 0 calories per gram = 0 calories). This makes sense. One shot of vodka is approximately 100 calories.

So now that we understand spirits, let's get back to the beer brain-buster.

If carbohydrates contain 4 calories per gram and alcohol contains 7 calories per gram, is low-carb beer more calorific than full-carb beer?

The answer is yes, sometimes. In order to understand this, we must review how beer is made.

Unlike hard alcohol, beer is not fully distilled. While the majority of the carbohydrate, barley, for example, is fermented to alcohol, some of it remains in carbohydrate form. This is why beer doesn't taste as strong as hard alcohol; it's sweeter and more filling. And this explains why many people have difficulty putting back straight vodka yet have no problem putting back straight beer. Beer contains three macronutrients: alcohol, carbohydrate and water.

To get a low-carb beer, one of the following two things has to happen:

1. The water content must be increased. If we keep the same size can of beer but make it higher in water, the alcohol and carb content remaining will naturally decrease. This trick has been known for a long time and is the recipe for many light beers. Coors Fine Light, for instance, is lower in carbs than regular beer because it has more water and therefore fewer carbohydrates and less alcohol. A bottle of light beer makes us less tipsy than a bottle of regular beer (because the former has less alcohol) and tastes lighter (because it has less carbohydrate and more water). Light beer is less calorific than traditional beer because it has more water; and water has zero calories.

2. The leftover carb content must be decreased. When the low-carb era began, beer companies jumped on the bandwagon and came up with a new way of making beer. The new method of 'mashing' carbs allows more of the carbs to be fermented to alcohol. These low-carb beers therefore often lack the flavour and body of regular beers. And guess what? They are more calorific because alcohol has nearly double the calories as regular carbohydrates, gram for gram.

Committed low-carb dieters have become so brainwashed by fancy marketing that they have forgotten the reason Dr. Atkins, the guru himself, swore off carbs in the first place. He blamed carbohydrates for today's obesity epidemic because carbs spike insulin levels. And, as you'll learn in Chapter 3, insulin is a fat-storing hormone.

On the Atkins diet, carbs are considered the enemy whereas fat and protein are encouraged because they are LESS likely to cause you to store fat. While there is some merit to this theory, the majority of low-carb dieters have completely missed the point. The advertising of alcohol as carb free or low carb exemplifies this point.

Alcohol raises insulin even more than carbohydrates! When we ingest alcohol, we absorb it into our blood very quickly. After all, as we've learned, alcohol is nothing more than fermented carbohydrates, and fermented carbohydrates raise insulin just like natural carbohydrates.

So alcohol is more calorific than carbohydrates and spikes our fat-storing insulin hormone as well. So who cares that alcohol is low in carbs? It would actually be better for us if it had more carbs and less alcohol: it'd be much better for us to eat straight barley (a fibrous complex carb) than fermented barley (an alcohol).

But for those – like me – who are not willing to forgo alcohol for life, don't worry. In Part Two, I have included a section on alcohol to show you how you can drink it while still losing weight and maintaining your health.

CHAPTER 2

The 'Hotty' Effect

The second important concept when it comes to weight loss is 'hotty' foods. 'Hotty' foods are so named because eating them encourages the body to heat up because calories are being burned! When we burn calories, heat is released. Read this again.

You see, simply by eating certain foods, you encourage your body to burn calories. This is because some foods are harder to digest and metabolise than others and, as a result, calories are burned. Consider eating these foods as exercise for your digestive tract! Before I go on to discuss what makes food 'hotty', let's take a minute to discuss the concept of calorie burning.

Every time your body works to heat itself up, you are burning calories. The more heat you make, the more calories you have burned. So an easy way to understand calorie burning and weight loss is to think about some of the things in life that cause us to heat up! Let's look at some of these now. (And no, putting on a jacket does not count!)

Exercise Exercise is certainly the most obvious thing that comes to mind. Think of what happens when we go for a jog or a bicycle ride, for instance. We heat up and start to sweat. Ever wonder why?

When we exercise, our bodies convert a stored form of energy into a form of energy that we can use for fuel. During this energy conversion, heat is released. Because we need to keep a constant body temperature, we quickly rid ourselves of this excess heat by sweating. As the perspiration evaporates, it cools us. So even though we're producing heat, our sweat glands protect us from overheating. Why is this important for weight loss? Well, the majority of energy is stored in the body as fat! It makes sense, then, that the more heat we produce, the more fat we burn! Actually, this is how metabolism can be measured. People are placed in water and those who create the most heat, causing the water to heat up the most, are said to have the fastest metabolism. The faster a person's metabolism is, the quicker her or she can convert fat into fuel and the more heat they produce in doing so. This is why people with fast metabolisms have an easier time staying thin.

So aside from giving you another reason to detest these fast-metabolizing skinny minnies, why should you care about this? Well, by understanding this concept, you can appreciate why exercise is so important for health and weight loss. Exercise increases metabolism and causes you to convert stored energy (fat) into usable energy (fuel). Now that you know that heat is the byproduct, you can't deny that exercise is critical for weight loss. Nothing causes you to sweat more, and therefore there is nothing better for burning calories, period. The next time you break a sweat, the next time you feel the 'burn', you know your effort will be rewarded by calories burned!

Any diet plan that says that exercise is not important is bogus. The more exercise you do, the more calories you will burn. You must get active to expedite weight loss! It doesn't matter what you do as long as you work up a sweat!

Resting metabolism Human beings are homeotherms. This means that humans try to maintain a constant body temperature, about 37°C (98.6°F), at all times no matter what their environment. This is why we feel sick when we have a fever. Our body temperature is not meant to go above this set point, so we feel shivery, sick and unwell. So how does the body keep this constant temperature? Well, one way is via our resting metabolism. Even when we aren't exercising, our bodies are converting food energy (the calories we consume from the food we eat) and/or stored energy (the calories of energy that are stored on our body as glycogen or fat) into usable energy (fuel) and the byproduct is heat. We don't feel sweaty at rest like we do when we exercise because we are doing this at a much slower rate and we need much less fuel when we are at rest. Sure, our heart still has to beat, our lungs have to breathe, our cells have to repair, but this is relatively easy compared to the mega work we have to do when running or cycling. So how can we force our bodies to work harder and therefore burn more calories when we are at rest? By having more lean muscle tissue.

Muscle cells take a lot of work to maintain compared to the other cells in the body. This means that two people who weigh the same amount, who eat the same amount of food and who both choose to laze around for the day doing nothing will burn a different number of calories depending on how much of their weight is made up of muscle. The 80-kilogram sprinter who is mostly muscle is a calorie-burning machine, whereas the 80-kilogram professional TV watcher who is mostly fat is burning very few calories. So what happens? The athlete gets thinner and the couch potato gets heavier, even though they're both sitting around doing nothing and eating the same amount of food! So the moral is that we must weight train and increase our muscle mass if we want to speed up our resting metabolism and burn more calories at rest. The best part is that after a session of weight training, our metabolism stays elevated because our muscles must work to repair themselves – burning even more calories!

Hormones Picture this: you hate public speaking. It's your brother's wedding and he's asked you to speak. You're up next. You're freaking out. Your heart is pounding. You can barely catch your breath. Your mouth feels dry. Your face is flushed. You're heating up. You're sweating buckets. Help! Is this familiar? Even if you love an audience and relish the opportunity to speak in public, everyone is stressed out by something, whether it is asking someone out on a date or getting caught in a lie. We've all felt these physical reactions and they manifest in the same ways for all of us. This is our fight-or-flight response, and it is triggered when we sense a potential threat. It's our sympathetic nervous system hormones – mainly adrenaline and its relative, noradrenaline – creating the physical reactions.

So why is this important when it comes to weight loss? Well, did you notice that part of this reaction involved sweating? These hormones can be thought of as fat-melting hormones. They are great at creating heat and burning calories! And while these hormones help us in times of stress, they're bad for us if released too often. However, there are ways to gently activate these hormones, thereby encouraging the body to burn calories without the negative consequences. The first is exercise. The second, however, is not as obvious: there are foods and drinks that can help us burn a few extra calories via this mechanism. You will learn about these in Phase One of the Hershberg Diet weight-loss plan.

Okay, so now that we understand how different methods of heating up can help us lose weight, let's look at one final way that our body is encouraged to burn calories: the thermogenic effect of food.

Thermogenic effect of food 'Thermo' means heat, as in a thermos or thermostat. 'Genic' means creating, as in genesis. So 'thermogenic' means heat-creating. The more heat we create after eating food, the more calories we burn off and the fewer we have available to store as fat! Some foods are very thermogenic, whereas others are not. By simply eating the right thermogenic foods, then, we can increase our metabolism and burn calories just by eating! From now on, I will refer to these calorie-burning, thermogenic foods as 'hotty' foods.

Of the three basic macronutrients, protein is the most 'hotty', followed by carbohydrates (complex carbs more so than simple carbs) and then, finally, fats. This means that our body must burn more calories to digest a high-protein meal than either a high-carb meal or a high-fat meal. Why? Well, proteins are big and complex molecules. The body must break these complex molecules down into simpler ones called amino acids before we can absorb and use them. This is hard work. So, when we eat [high-protein foods, such as turkey, chicken, fish and seafood, for example] we burn calories, thus releasing heat. Protein is 'hotty'!

Complex fibrous carbohydrates are the next best at burning calories. Remember from Chapter 1 that the more sugar molecules that are linked together to form a carbohydrate, the more complex the carbohydrate is said to be? We must break down all carbohydrates to glucose (sugar) before the body can absorb and use them. Knowing this, it makes sense that complex carbs are more 'hotty' than simple carbs; it takes more work to break them down to glucose and therefore burns more calories in the process. Complex high-fibre carbohydrates (like wholegrain bread, brown rice and oatmeal, for example) are like complex literature: it takes a long time to digest the material, but once you do, the effort is rewarded! Complex high-fibre carbs are 'hotty'!

Simple and low-fibre carbs (like sweets and processed refined snack foods – crisps, biscuits, white bread, white rice and sugary cereals, for example) are simple to digest and, as a result, the work is not as rewarded by calories burned. Simple and low-fibre carbs are therefore not 'hotty'.

Fat is the least 'hotty' of the basic macronutrients. Before fat can enter our bloodstream, it must be digested to fatty acids and glycerol. As you may have guessed, this is done easily and few calories are burned as a result. But there's a catch. The process is also done quite slowly. Although we aren't burning very many calories, we are staying quite full because it takes a long time for the digestive process to complete. Fats therefore fill us up. When we eat fat along with the other macronutrients, it can actually help us by slowing the rate at which the whole meal is absorbed. So while fat is the least 'hotty', don't cut it out of your diet just yet.

On the Hershberg Diet plan, I will show you which foods to eat and how to eat them so that you capitalize on all these pros while avoiding the cons.

Let's review what we have learned so far:

- Get active to burn calories. Breaking a sweat means burning calories. That's why you feel hot when you exercise!
- Build muscle to speed up resting metabolism. Maintaining a muscle cell is harder work than for any other cell and, as a result, calories are burned. The more muscle you have, the more calories you will burn at rest. You will also burn extra calories following a session of weight training because your body is still working hard to build and repair the muscle fibres. If you feel the burn, smile, because you're burning calories!
- Activating the right hormones can help you burn calories. You will learn more about this in the next chapter. You will also learn which foods to eat to gently stimulate these hormones.
- In terms of calorie-burning 'hotty' foods, protein are the most 'hotty', then complex high-fibre carbs then low-fibre simple carbs, then fat.

Okay, let's go on to Chapter 3. Once you complete this final introductory chapter, you are ready for The Hershberg Diet weight-loss plan.

The Hormonal Effect

Now that we understand how the 'fourth macronutrient' (water) and thermogenesis ('hotty' foods) contribute to weight loss, we are ready to tackle the third and final concept – the hormonal effect.

In this chapter, you will learn how to create the optimal hormonal environment for weight loss. In addition to helping prevent cardiovascular disease and diabetes, the information you will learn will help you understand why you may be gaining weight despite eating very little food. The explanation almost always resides in the body's response to insulin.

So what is insulin?

Insulin is a hormone made by the pancreas. It is an incredibly important hormone as, without it, we could not live. Insulin allows sugar (remember, all carbohydrates are digested to sugar) to move from our bloodstreams into our cells. Once the sugar enters our cells, it undergoes a process called cellular respiration in order to make fuel ('cellular' because it's in our cells, and 'respiration' because it requires that we breathe in oxygen and breathe out carbon dioxide). Without this fuel, we could not function; we would be like a car without petrol. So insulin is a very important hormone. But insulin also signals the body to store fat, a process called lipogenesis. You see, sugar can easily be converted to fat instead of fuel. Why? Well, think of your body as a car again.

What do you do when your car's petrol gauge approaches empty? You start to look for the nearest petrol station for a fill-up, right? Well, when the fuel in the body runs low, the body starts to think about how it will get its next fill-up. Of course, we could eat food, but in the past, food was not always readily available. We had to be able to have a backup method, and we do. Remember from last chapter that we have energy stored on the body that is capable of making fuel. Energy is stored on our hips, thighs, bellies, etc. as fat, and it's also stored in the muscle and liver as glycogen, a type of carbohydrate. Like food, the fat on the body contains about 9 calories of energy per gram and the carbohydrate (glycogen) in the muscle and liver has about 4 calories of energy per gram. So if we can't eat to fill up, we simply break down these stores and release the energy. Insulin is the hormone that allows us to store energy (fat) on the body for later use.

When we eat a meal, we use some of the sugar (remember, all carbohydrates break down to sugar) for fuel, but if we have some left over, we store it for later. The insulin allows the sugar to get into all of our cells and, if it's not used right away for fuel, it will be converted to glycogen or fat and stored for later use.

Certain foods cause sugar to move into our bloodstreams too quickly. Then lots of insulin is released and some fuel is made – but there is a lot of leftover sugar to deal with. We get a sugar spike followed by an insulin spike followed by fat deposition followed by a crash in blood sugar. Now the situation worsens. When blood sugar levels are low, our brain thinks that we are starving; that we need more food, more sugar. So we incorrectly feel hungry and then seek out more food ... more food that we'll simply store as fat! We feel hungry but for the wrong reason. We don't need more fuel; we have incorrectly caused our blood sugar levels to plummet because we ate unnatural sugar-spiking foods.

When we overeat sugar-spiking foods, we over-release insulin and we store too much fat. But the body is smart; it tries to protect us from overeating by rejecting the insulin! This is how insulin resistance, the precursor to diabetes, develops. **FYI**, if your doctor has told you that you are 'pre-diabetic' or have 'insulin resistance', this is likely to be what's happening within your body. At this stage, if you start watching your eating and changing your food habits, the situation may be reversible. However, this is not what the majority of us do.

When we don't change our eating habits, we force the pancreas to give us more insulin. We encounter a situation called hyperinsulinemia (high insulin levels in the blood), which is how the body tries to beat the insulin resistance. And it works – for a little while. The problem is that now we are en route to becoming significantly overweight and diabetic. Let's look at why.

Although we have more insulin around, it doesn't work nearly as well as it used to. So some sugar stays trapped in our blood, unable to enter our cells. This is why we start to develop chronically high blood sugar levels irrespective of whether we've eaten. **FYI**, this is the reason that doctors order *fasting* blood work; they want to see how high your blood sugar level is when you haven't eaten. If your blood sugar is high, the doctor knows that the hormonal situation in your body is not optimal. Even worse, these chronically high blood sugar levels trick the pancreas into thinking that we need even more insulin. Remember, it is insulin's job to clear the sugar from the blood by allowing it to enter our cells. So now, with insulin not working properly, we always have high blood sugar levels, we always want more insulin to help clear them, and we are always in a state of telling our bodies to store fat, even when we haven't eaten! Believe it or not, the situation gets even worse.

For fat loss to occur, the body likes insulin levels to be low. When insulin levels are low, the body thinks that blood sugar must be getting too low, and if blood sugar is low, the body quickly uses its fat and glycogen stores to make fuel. So low insulin levels are associated with fat loss. When insulin levels are low, certain special hormones (including the adrenaline and noradrenaline discussed in Chapter 2) are signalled to fire. These hormones signal our body fat stores to turn into fuel and heat.

People often think that overweight people who claim to be dieting and not losing weight are lying. How can they be consuming so little and not losing weight? Now you know how! Having eaten too many of the wrong sugar-spiking foods in the past, they created a situation of chronically high blood sugar and insulin. As a result, the body is constantly in a state of thinking that it must either need to make fuel or store fat, because why else would sugar and insulin levels be high? You see, overeating sugar-spiking foods creates a situation whereby you gain weight easily even when you're not eating very much. It's like going further and further into debt even when you're not spending money – simply because the interest is accumulating.

To add insult to injury, the chronically high insulin levels discourage fat-melting hormones from firing! It is no wonder that the ambitious dieter is not losing weight. How could he when his body is in a constant state of wanting to accumulate fat and not wanting to burn it?

It is at this point that family doctors often detect early diabetes. Through screening of urine or blood, a high sugar level is found. The first line of treatment is diet; unfortunately, people are often not told that it must be a diet that discourages blood sugar and insulin levels from spiking. It must be a diet that recruits the fat-burning hormones. It must be a diet that prevents metabolism from slowing. Finally, it must be a diet that is filling, palatable, nutritious and sustainable.

The Hershberg Diet weight-loss plan meets all of these criteria. It is easy to follow and medically sound. The foods that are promoted help stabilize insulin and blood sugar levels. Through eating these foods, nutrients will be absorbed slowly into the bloodstream. This controlled release will prevent blood sugar and insulin spikes. Fat-burning hormones will be activated not only through this lowering of insulin levels but also by the use of 'hotty' foods. 'Hotty' foods can gently stimulate these fat-melting hormones, adding additional ammunition for your fat-loss goal. The diet is sustainable; you are encouraged to eat foods from all of the macronutrient categories and even allowed to indulge any of your cravings, provided that you follow the techniques taught in the next section. It is through these healthy eating habits that we will win the fight against obesity, insulin resistance and diabetes and beat the Syndrome once and for all.

Let's review the major concepts introduced in this section:

- Insulin promotes sugar uptake into cells and its conversion to fuel and heat, with leftovers being stored largely as fat.
- High insulin levels can cause us to accumulate fat easily, even when we haven't eaten!
- Foods that spike blood sugar and insulin levels encourage the situation of fat storage as opposed to fat melting.
- Chronically high blood sugar and insulin levels discourage the release of fat-melting hormones.
- Eating foods that prevent spikes in blood sugar and insulin levels will help create an optimal environment for weight loss.

Fad Diets Analysed

We live in a fast-paced world. We crave immediacy, high speed and instantaneous results. We want instant oatmeal, instant rice, immediate service and fast food. We want high-speed Internet banking, automatic cash-machines and instant wealth. While we seek speedy results when it comes to both our weight and our wealth, we use better judgment when it comes to the latter. Whereas we are sceptical of get-rich-quick schemes, we fall for fad diet after fad diet, without ever taking the time to question the underlying rationales.

As you'll see, many popular fad diets are founded on flawed science. While they may work for the short term, their restrictive nature often makes them unsustainable. More importantly, their flawed reasoning can set us up for weight gain and at times even harm our health. Let's take a closer look at these dietary 'get-rich-quick schemes'.

Low-Fat Diet

When an entire category of macronutrient is severely restricted from our diets, the result will initially and intuitively be calorie reduction and thus weight loss, unless a substitute is introduced.

Low-fat eating sounds like a nutritionally sound and appropriate solution to the emerging obesity problem. At 9 calories per gram, fat costs twice as many calories as either protein or carbohydrates. Remember from

Chapter 1 that fat is hydrophobic, meaning that what you see is what you get in terms of portion (there are no zero-calorie water grams to expand the portion). Ten grams of oil is therefore 90 calories (10 grams × 9 calories per gram = 90 calories). A very low-fat diet certainly seems reasonable because by cutting out fat, we'd be cutting out the most calorific part of our diets. Also, as most snack foods, baked goods and protein and dairy products contain fat, our food options would be seriously limited. We would have to rely on lean meats, fish, fruits, vegetables, potatoes, pasta, rice and breads. Sounds good, right? Well, let's look at what happens.

Because all types of fat are condemned on low-fat diets, cooking meats and fish becomes challenging. So people on these diets tend to eat foods that are very high in carbohydrates, low in protein and low in fat. As we've seen, these type of foods, such as bagels, crispbreads and cereals, are almost purely dry carbohydrate (i.e., they contain virtually no water). As a result, they are not very filling, and it is easy to eat much more than the recommended single portion size (half a bagel, four crispbreads, one slice of bread, etc.) without feeling full. Further, because these foods are labeled 'fat-free' and thus incorrectly interpreted as 'calorie-free' by the majority of the population, people eat gargantuan portion sizes, thereby defying the initial plan of cutting calories.

As the low-fat craze caught on, the market became saturated with reduced-fat and fat-free foods. Food scientists teamed with corporate business to remove fat from foods and replace it with the next tastiest thing – sugar! Now people were loading up on reduced-fat biscuits, crisps, cakes, ice creams, etc. Although the low-fat replacements were slightly lower in calories than their original forms because sugar has 4 calories to fat's 9 calories per gram, people were more than making up for this difference by increasing portion sizes, thinking that only the fat grams mattered. The prevailing sentiment of the time was, 'Calories don't make you fat, fat makes you fat.' Unfortunately, as many of us know, this thinking proved completely wrong.

As many of you ex-low-fat dieters know, the result of the low-fat craze for many people was weight gain! People consumed excess calories in the form of fat-free carbohydrates (bagels, sweets, rice cakes) and gained weight. Even worse, as most of these high-carb, low-fat foods are dry, with little water weight to expand their volume, people were packing on the pounds while still feeling hungry! Insulin levels surged, stimulating appetite, and the low water content didn't fill us up. Fortunately, people started to wise up and say goodbye to fat-free eating. However, it was only a matter of time before history repeated itself – low-carb Britain was born.

Very Low-Carbohydrate Diet

Low-carb diets are not new and actually work a lot like the 'carb-loading' that marathon runners used to do before a big race. The two sound like opposites, but they're not.

Before a big race, marathon runners would often deplete their carbohydrate stores by eating only fat and protein – think steak, cheese, eggs – a week before the race. By eliminating carbs from the diet, the dedicated runner forced his body to draw upon its stored form of carbohydrate – glycogen. (Recall from Chapter 3 that glycogen is a type of carbohydrate that we keep stored in our liver and muscles for emergency energy purposes. This way, when blood sugar or energy is too low, as occurs when we avoid eating carbs, we can quickly convert glycogen into glucose (sugar) and continue functioning.) Now glycogen, like all carbs, is hydrophilic ('hydro' = water; 'philic' = loving). This means that it is attracted to water and absorbs it. So the carb-starved athlete would go into a state of glycogen depletion and, for each gram of glycogen lost from his muscle, he'd lose approximately 3 grams of body water along with it. The result was a strategically shrunken, dehydrated body perfectly prepped to rapidly increase in size when the athlete began carb-loading.

You see, a few days before the big race, the athlete would load up on high-carb foods such as pasta and bread. The hungry muscles would get very excited that carbohydrates were once again available, so they would eat them up very efficiently. The glycogen and water were replaced quickly and efficiently, and the runner's muscles could now serve as big, bulky, volume-expanded energy reserves capable of sustaining his energy needs throughout the race.

Most athletes have stopped doing this, though, because the quick water gain was painful to their muscles. In fact, the quick increase in water made it more difficult for the oxygen in the blood to get to the muscle cells. Without oxygen, our cells can make only lactic acid. Increased lactic acid and decreased fuel leads to burning pain and, ultimately, cell death. The scariest part is that this can occur in the heart muscle as well. When a heart doesn't get enough oxygen, this is a heart attack. Now let's see how this is similar to the very low-carbohydrate diet.

In the induction phase of low-carb diets, most carbohydrates are severely restricted, even healthy and 'hotty' ones like complex carbohydrates, fruits and most vegetables. This carbohydrate depletion scares the body into rapidly converting the stored glycogen in the liver and muscle into glucose. Remember, this shrinks the size of the muscles because water is lost with the glycogen. So the satisfying visible weight loss seen at the beginning of these diets is actually mostly water weight!

Once glycogen is used up, the body is forced to use fat and protein sources to make sugar and ketones, an alternative source of fuel. The body is now in 'ketosis', which can be very dangerous, especially when combined with dehydration. Thankfully, this potentially dangerous ketotic state is very difficult to sustain. After all, it requires that you stick quite rigidly to a very low-carbohydrate diet.

How many people do you know who have stuck with an extremely low-carbohydrate diet? Not many. It's hard to fight our biochemistry. Often, people stick with it for a month or so. They lose fat, probably about 1 to 2 pounds per week as they are restricting their calories. After all, it's hard not to lose weight when you are restricting an entire macronutrient category (carbohydrates), especially the one that constitutes most snack foods, desserts and sweets. In addition, people on very low-carb diets lose water, muscle and bone weight. Delighted with their impressive weight loss, they loosen their restriction and indulge in carbohydrates. Just like the carb-loader marathon runner whose muscles were initially starved, the body now becomes superefficient at storing any consumed sugars. The result: rapid, excessive, and potentially dangerous bloating and weight gain, if muscle cells can't get enough oxygen. If you recall the example of the carb-loader marathon runner I gave earlier, you'll remember that when muscles quickly increase in size from the replacement of glycogen and water, it makes it difficult for the cells to get enough oxygen. And without oxygen, cells die. In the heart muscle, for example, this is called a heart attack or myocardial (heart muscle) infarction (death due to lack of oxygen). So most people regain the weight quickly, only to set themselves up for an even more challenging weight loss the next time around. (Each time we lose weight quickly and then gain it back, we lose lean muscle weight and replace it with fat because it's easier to rebuild fat stores than muscles. As we know from Chapter 2, muscle burns more calories than fat, so the result is less lean muscle tissue, more fat and slower metabolisms.)

Have you ever heard of a 'fat skinny' person? Are you a 'fat skinny' person? 'Fat skinnies' are created through this process of repeated fad dieting and are people who may not weigh much because they have less muscle, water and bone weight, but they have high percentages of body fat. 'Fat skinnies' may be a size 4, but they don't look nearly as good as a size 4 made of lean muscle tissue and water, and they certainly aren't as healthy. It is perpetual yo-yo dieting that sets people up to become 'fat skinnies'.

Cyclic weight loss and gain isn't the only problem with these diets. In addition, by eliminating carbohydrates, we deprive ourselves of some very healthy and 'hotty' foods: fibre, for instance. Although most green vegetables are permitted on low-carb diets, fruit and grain sources of fibre are limited, which increases our risk of constipation, bowel disorders and some cancers. Also, we miss out on the calorie-burning potential of these foods. Remember from Chapter 2 that breaking down complex fibrous carbohydrates burns a lot of calories as heat. Further, when our bodies digest high-water fibrous carbohydrates, sugars are released into the blood in a controlled fashion. This prevents us from having to break down our muscle and tissue proteins for fuel. As you can see, there are serious problems associated with very low-carbohydrate diets.

Although very low-carbohydrate diets are flawed, we can still learn from them. These diets unintentionally promote the water properties of food. By virtually eliminating one of the three macronutrients from the diet, we are theoretically left with only two-thirds the amount of choice (protein and fat). Once you remove the carbohydrate-rich foods, you are left with meat, fish and some dairy, fruit and vegetables. Essentially, high-water foods!

You see, the secret to the real and lasting weight loss is not carb deprivation but, rather, committing to a diet of high-water foods!

The Glycemic Index (GI)
This concept has caught on quickly and is now being used widely by medical professionals to counsel their

patients on healthy eating. Typically, patients are told that eating a diet of low-GI foods will help prevent diabetes and help them lose weight; they are then sent off to figure out what on earth this means and how they can use it to select healthy foods.

The obsession with a food's GI comes from advances in knowledge of insulin and its effect on hunger, weight and energy levels as well as the unavoidable reality that we are being faced with an epidemic of diabetes. So what is the GI?

The GI is a ranking of carbohydrates on a scale from zero to 100 according to the rate at which they raise blood sugar levels after eating. Specifically, the GI of a food is assessed by comparing 50 grams of the digestible available carbohydrate component of that food with 50 grams of glucose (a very simple sugar) to see how similar they act in terms of raising blood sugar levels. The closer the food acts to glucose, the higher its GI rating will be and the worse for you it is considered to be. So foods with a high GI, such as sweets and white bread, quickly raise blood sugar levels whereas foods with a low GI, like oatmeal, raise blood sugar levels more slowly. While this theory certainly sounds scientific and meritorious, let's see how it stands up to closer analysis.

To fully understand the GI, we must first look at what is meant by the phrase 'digestible carbohydrate'. Not all carbohydrates are digestible. Fibre is defined as an indigestible carbohydrate because it passes through the stomach and intestines without being digested; it provides bulk and therefore helps us stay regular. So because the GI of a food is assessed by comparing 50 grams of the digestible available carbohydrate component of that food with 50 grams of glucose, we must subtract the fat, protein, water and fibre content of the food to arrive at the actual digestible carbohydrate component leftover. (Remember that fat, protein, water and fibre aren't digestible carbohydrates – only carbohydrates are carbohydrates.) Are you still with me? This is where the flaws inherent with using the GI system become apparent.

When we eat meals, we do not subtract the protein, fat, fibre and water content of the food and select portion sizes based on how much digestible carbohydrate is left over. The GI, while useful in theory, does not make sense when it comes to actual eating in real life. Let's take eating an apple as an example.

To arrive at the correct GI of an apple, we'd have to peel it (take out the fibre), then dehydrate it (take out the water), and then eat 50 grams of what's left over to get at the digestible carbohydrate component and therefore the proper GI. Is this how the majority of us eat apples? NO! We bite into them through their peels and enjoy their watery/juicy goodness. Because we're consuming the fibre and the water, we're actually eating fewer than '50 grams of digestible carbohydrate', so more than one apple must be eaten to arrive at the correct GI value.

Next, let's look at carrots. As some of you may know, carrots have received a bad name in recent years. Both the Atkins and South Beach diets consider them to be too high in carbs to be eaten regularly when trying to lose weight. And now even the health-conscious GI dieters are avoiding this veggie as it has been rated as a very high-GI food. But based on what I have just taught, this just isn't the case.

Carrots are high in fibre and water, and are difficult to consume with the fibre and water extracted. To arrive at 50 grams of 'digestible carbohydrate', then, a person would have to eat roughly an entire bag of baby carrots! So the GI value of carrots is likely based on an entire bag. But we don't eat carrots this way. We munch on a handful or two as a snack or shred some into a salad. When it comes to assessing high-water, high-fibre foods like carrots, the portions used are much bigger than one would typically consume. This is why green vegetables, which are very high in water and fibre, don't even have GI values! The testers would literally have had to have eaten several bags of them to finally consume the required '50 grams of digestible carbohydrate', so it just wasn't done.

Now close your eyes and think of various foods that we consume excessively that have virtually no water, fibre, protein or fat. For me, sliced white bread, sugar cereals, fat-free sweets and biscuits came to mind. For these foods, the GI is bang on because, unlike the peeling and dehydrating we have to do to arrive at the correct GI of an apple, we can just eat these foods as they are, no subtracting necessary!

To summarize, then, the first flaw with the GI has to do with the equivalency system (i.e., arriving at the 50-gram 'digestible carbohydrate' component). Dry refined foods that are low in fibre and water have GI values that make sense, and for these types of food, the GI is an excellent and important tool. However, foods that are high in fibre and water, such as fruits and veg, often have GI values that are falsely higher than they should be.

Let's have a look at flaw number two. When

measuring the GI, we are measuring how similar the test food is to pure glucose in terms of raising blood sugar levels. If a food raises blood sugar levels quickly, it is given a high GI and is considered to be bad for us. If a food raises blood sugar levels slowly, it is given a lower GI and is considered to be better for us. But does this make sense?

Recall that fat slows the rate at which sugar is digested into our bloodstream. Fatty foods sit in our stomachs for a long time before being digested, which is why they are filling. If carbohydrates are mixed with fat, then it is harder for the digestive enzymes to get at the carbohydrate, and the sugars are therefore absorbed more slowly. Thus, the more fat a carbohydrate food contains, the lower its GI. So a piece of heavily buttered toast (i.e., fat mixed with carbohydrate) will have a lower GI than a piece of plain toast without the added fat! Read this again. Surely this does not mean that buttered toast is better for us than plain toast, or does it?

Let's look at another example, crisps. Crisps have a lower GI than watermelon! We all know that fat-laden crisps are not healthier than watermelon, so why the lower GI? Because watermelon is high in water and low in fat. The qualities that render this fruit a healthy choice intuitively are the same qualities that give it a high, and therefore unhealthy, GI rating. Long story short: the GI system is flawed.

Years of research and personal experiences have shown us that high-fat diets are linked to weight gain, diabetes, heart disease and cancers. You just don't see athletes walking around devouring crisps and swearing off fruits and vegetables, now, do you?

GI values also don't differentiate between different types of fat! For instance, which is better, olive oil or butter? GI values won't tell us. As you can see, eating solely based on the GI value of foods is not a good approach to weight loss and health promotion.

Finally, and most importantly, the GI system does not reflect how people eat normally. We don't eat portion sizes of carbohydrate foods based on the fibre, fat, protein and water being factored out. Further, we don't eat foods in isolation. As soon as we combine one food with another, as we do when we eat meals, the GI values are no longer accurate as the ratio of fats, proteins and carbohydrates become altered.

Now that we have reviewed the popular diets, we can appreciate the factor that links the merits of all of them. WATER! Further, we can see that when diets fail to appreciate the water content of food, they don't work. The Hershberg Diet, with its emphasis on this vital 'fourth macronutrient' and 'hotty' properties, will help get us back on track.

PART TWO

The Hershberg Diet Weight-Loss Plan

CHAPTER 4

Let's Review

Congratulations! You have made it to Part Two. You'll now learn how the three concepts taught in Part One can be combined to create an easy, delicious and sustainable weight-loss plan. First, let's quickly review these three concepts:

1. **The 'Fourth Macronutrient'**   Water is the 'fourth macronutrient'. It is a critical, often-forgotten component of food, yet must be considered for weight loss. The more water a food contains, the better it is for weight loss. This concept was explained in Chapter 1.

2. **The 'Hotty' Effect** 'Hotty' foods are excellent for weight loss because eating these foods encourages the body to heat up and burn calories. Incorporating 'hotty' foods into our diets will

help us lose weight. Some 'hotty' foods can even activate fat-melting hormones. This concept was explained in Chapter 2.

3. **The Hormonal Effect** When overeaten or eaten improperly, foods that spike blood sugar and insulin levels can create a hormonal situation in the body that encourages the body to store fat, even when you're not eating. For optimal weight loss, you must eat a diet that encourages the body to handle insulin properly and activates hormones that promote weight loss. This concept was explained in Chapter 3.

CHAPTER 5

Alcohol

Before we get started, let's discuss how alcohol fits into the Hershberg Diet weight-loss plan.

Alcohol certainly isn't a dieter's best friend (think of a 'beer belly'). But the Hershberg Diet is not about deprivation; it is meant to be easy to implement and sustain. You can drink alcohol on this diet plan as long as you have appropriate strategies to ensure that you do not jeopardise your weight-loss goals.

Using your knowledge of the three concepts introduced thus far, you'll know that the best foods and drinks for weight loss are those that are high in water, are 'hotty', and have the right hormonal effect. How does alcohol rate?

Alcohol causes us to lose water. It inhibits the hormone that causes us to hold onto water. This is why we make so many bathroom trips when we drink alcohol! This is also why we feel hungover and dehydrated following a night of drinking. So when drinking alcohol, we must increase the water factor. Forgo mixed drinks completely, as most mixers are either concentrated sugar or fat. Or simply drink your beverage on the rocks or mixed with water. If you must have a mixed drink, choose a vegetable juice mixer such as V8 or tomato juice. Also, drink a glass of water for every alcoholic drink consumed.

Alcohol can cause unstable blood sugar levels. In fact, it can spike and drop blood sugar levels rapidly and excessively. This is one reason why we crave so many simple high-sugar carbohydrates (crisps, chips, pizza, etc.) when we drink! Our bodies are probably trying to quickly raise our blood sugar levels back up to normal. As you can see, when we add the calories consumed from drinking with the calories consumed from these foods, it's no surprise that weight gain often ensues! To combat this, drink alcohol slowly following a meal that contains some starchy carbohydrates such as wholemeal breads, pasta, rice or legumes. *Do not* skip dinner or skimp on carbs before drinking; it will not save calories but will set you up for a late night high-sugar binge! The other trick that you may use when drinking is one that the stars often use, or so I've heard, to make it through a long night of drinking at an awards show or event. Swallow 1 tablespoon of olive or flaxseed oil (or take two flaxseed or fish oil supplements) before drinking. The fat will slow the rate of alcohol absorption; you will crave fewer high-sugar foods and feel less hungover the following day.

Alcohol may cause us to confuse what's 'hotty' and what's not. To increase the 'hotty' potential when drinking, get active. Dance! This way you will burn off some of the calories that you are consuming.

Most importantly, drink in moderation! While it is best to limit alcohol as much as possible when trying to lose weight, if you must imbibe, it is suggested that you limit your consumption.

TIPS

- Say no to all sugary and fatty mixed drinks.
- Wine and light beers are good options.
- Drink a glass of water for every alcoholic drink consumed.
- Do not skip dinner or skimp on carbohydrates before drinking.
- Consume complex carbohydrates (like the ones that will be introduced in Phase Two) before or along with alcohol or have 1 tablespoon (15 mL) of olive or flaxseed oil (or two fish oil or flaxseed oil supplements) before drinking.

If you follow these rules, you should be able to enjoy alcohol without compromising your weight-loss and health goals.

Now you are ready to embark on the the Hershberg Diet weight-loss plan. You will learn how to use the three concepts for optimal weight loss and health. This information will change the way you approach food and eating for life!

The Initiation Phase

Phase One is a two-week initiation phase. It is the strictest phase of the diet and is designed to cleanse your body and jump-start weight loss. Foods high in the 'fourth macronutrient' are emphasized in this phase. So in this phase your diet will consist mostly of high-water fruits, vegetables, dairy products, fish, chicken and meats. Because the foods suggested are high in water and therefore the best for weight loss, I encourage you to eat as much as you need to feel full and satisfied. There is no counting or tracking required. That said, your meals should still be of reasonable size, enough to satisfy your hunger but no more than that. You should feel comfortable following meals, not bursting or overstuffed.

Read the list of 'Foods to Enjoy in Phase One' carefully. Stock your fridge, freezer and cupboards with these foods so that you always have them on hand. These foods should always make up the majority of your diet, no matter which phase you are in.

After you become familiar with the list of Phase One foods, read the information that follows on their associated health benefits and weight-loss properties.

In the following sections, you will find an extensive collection of easy-to-make and delicious recipes as well as a sample 14-day menu plan. You can follow the meal plan exactly for two weeks or simply use it for meal ideas.

By the time the phase ends, you will notice a significant change in your body; unhealthy high-sugar cravings will be reduced and

Contrary to intuition, eating high-water foods results in body water loss (diuresis) as opposed to body water gain (swelling). Here's an easy way to understand this principle.

Our bodies must keep the concentration of solutes, such as sodium and potassium, incredibly stable. This is done by altering the amount of solvent – body water. Think about it: if you put a tablespoon of salt in a glass of water, what's the easiest way to make it taste saltier? By pouring out some of the water – this increases the concentration of salt (sodium). Now, because water plays such an important role in regulating solute concentrations, our bodies store excess water for this purpose (in our ankles, hands, hips, bellies, etc.) just in case it's not available from our diets. So just like our bodies are designed to store fat to protect us from starvation, our bodies store water to protect us from dehydration. Now, when the majority of our diets consist of high-water foods, the body senses that it is at no threat of dehydration, so it feels confident that it can shed some of the extra water that it had been storing. The result? Eating high-water foods will help you lose excess water weight – you feel thinner, less bloated and your blood pressure decreases.

your body will already begin to look and feel better as fat is lost and water retention decreases.

Foods to Enjoy in Phase One

While all of the following foods qualify as acceptable for Phase One, I separated them into two columns. This is because the foods in the left column are so high in water and so good for weight loss that they deserve special attention. Make your selections from this column as often as possible to speed weight loss!

Veggies – asparagus, bok choy, broccoli, brussels sprouts, burdock, celery, courgettes, cucumber, endive, green beans, green onion, mangetout, kale, leeks, lettuce, pickles (not sweet varieties), spring greens, spring onions, spinach, vegetable consomme, all herbs	**Veggies** – artichokes, aubergines, beets, red and green peppers, carrots, cauliflower, fennel, mushrooms, okra, olives, onion, pumpkin, raddish, rhubarb, swede, squash, Swiss chard, taro root, tomatoes, tomato sauce (no sugar added), watercress, yellow beans
Fruits – lemon, lime, all berries, grapefruit	**Fruits** – apple, avocado, banana, cantaloupe, cherries, grapes, guava, honeydew, kiwi, kumquat, loquat, nectarine, orange, papaya, passion fruit, peach, pear, persimmon, pineapple, plum, tangerine, watermelon, unsweetened apple sauce, fruit-flavoured sugar-free jelly

Animal protein – egg whites (or low-fat liquid egg substitutes); beef or chicken consomme	**Animal protein** – chicken and turkey without skin (white meat); fish and seafood (those packed in oil, battered, deep fried, or mixed with butter/cream sauce don't count); lean cuts of red meat (pork, veal, beef, lamb) trimmed of fat; back bacon; lean ground chicken and turkey; lean turkey, cooked pre-packed chicken and ham slices; game meat
Vegetable protein – vegetable consomme; miso soup	**Vegetable protein** – tofu (buy low-fat varieties); low-fat veggie-based meat substitutes, burgers and sausages; sugar-free low-fat soy and whey-based protein powders and drinks
Dairy – none	**Dairy** – low-fat milk and soy milk (skimmed is best); fat-free, artificially sweetened yogurts (not frozen varieties); fat-free or reduced-fat cottage cheese, ricotta or feta; reduced-fat soured cream; fat-free, artificially sweetened frozen treats (must have fewer than 50 calories per bar)

Drinks – water, green tea, black tea	**Drinks** – vegetable juice, light or diet fruit-flavoured juice, diet hot chocolate, coffee, diet soft drinks
Fats – fat-free, low-calorie cooking spray	**Fats** – olive oil, flaxseed oil, rapeseed oil, vegetable oil, sesame oil, safflower oil, sunflower oil, non-hydrogenated light margarine, reduced-fat salad dressings, reduced-fat mayonnaise

Extras Chillies, mustard, cinnamon, garlic, ginger, vinegars, soy sauce, sugar substitutes, any other herb or spice (including seasoning salts)

Vegetables As you may recall from our romaine lettuce example in Chapter 1, most vegetables can be considered 'waters' because so much of their weight is made up of zero-calorie water! Additionally, many vegetables contain fibre. We must work to digest that fibre, which burns calories. Most vegetables, provided they are not cooked with fat or dipped in fatty or sugary sauces, can help us lose weight just by eating them. If that's not hot, I don't know what is! Stock your fridge, freezer and kitchen cupboards with fresh, frozen and canned vegetables and include them in meals and snacks as often as possible.

TIPS

- Eat vegetables raw, steamed or boiled to preserve water content.
- Consume salads with meals as a side dish rather than before the meal. You will eat much less this way and your meal will be more satisfying.
- The vegetables in the left column of the preceding chart are especially high in water. When you eat them, you may even burn more calories than you consume! Include these in meals as often as possible to maximise weight loss.
- Asparagus, cucumber and parsley are excellent natural mild diuretics that can help us shed water weight.
- Pickled vegetables are virtually calorie-free, although they do contain a lot of salt. Too much salt can make you bloat, so be careful!
- Olives are higher in fat and salt than most other vegetables, but they are extremely nutritious. Unless you eat them in excessive quantities, olives (less than five per serving) can be part of any smart weight-loss plan!
- My new favourite vegetable is spaghetti squash. It is the perfect substitute for pasta, hence its name! I make dishes like squash pizza (I use a layer of baked squash instead of dough). I make a delicious squash lasagna – and even squash pie! Read the following recipe section to learn how to use this wonder veggie. Although it is slightly more calorific than some other vegetables, it is more filling and therefore the perfect replacement for low-water, low-'hotty' and insulin-spiking starches such as white bread, pasta and rice.
- We know that tomatoes are high in water and excellent

for weight loss. As well as this, a substance in tomatoes called lycopene has also been shown to help fight prostate cancer, the most common cancer in men.

- Be careful when consuming canned vegetable soups and sauces, as many of them contain plenty of added sugar and salt. Check the ingredient list or nutrition label to ensure that sugar isn't on the list, or simply make your own.

Fruits If you are among the many people who avoided fruits, erroneously thinking that they were too high in sugar to facilitate weight loss, get ready to enjoy these sweet natural delicacies again. Fruits are among the highest-water, -fibre, and '-hotty' foods around – so they can help us lose weight! You will be amazed at how good you start to feel when you incorporate fruit into your diet. Even better, your craving for high-sugar junk foods will drastically diminish as you include fruit in your diet. Because fruit can be higher in sugar than the other Phase One foods, I suggest you have **no more than 2 per day** when choosing from the right column.

While whole fruits help with weight loss, fruit juices do not! Juices are higher in sugar because many fruits have to be sqeezed to get the juice – when we eat the fruit, we eat the juice plus the high-fibre peel, rind and seeds. The juice lacks the fibre and 'hotty' properties of the fruits from which they are made. When we take the fibre out, we speed the absorption of sugar into our blood. Eat the fruit; ditch the juice!

Dried fruits are low-water. (They are dried!) They are therefore very concentrated forms of sugar and calories and should be avoided. Sorry, but no raisins, dried cranberries or any other dried fruit that you can think of allowed in Phase One.

TIPS

- Lemons and limes are acidic citrus fruits. Acid helps slow the absorption of sugar into the blood and thus helps to create the proper hormonal effect. Also, these foods are so high in water that they can be considered calorie-free! Squeeze lemons and limes into water and tea and over foods to maximize weight loss.

- Berries contain a lot of water and insoluble (indigestible) fibre. They are therefore among the lowest-calorie foods. Berries must be eaten fresh or frozen and never dried or with added sugar.

- As you may recall from Chapter 1, grapefruit is essentially a water with fibre. Sweeten it with a sugar substitute such as Splenda or stevia (a natural sweetener) mixed with cinnamon to maintain the 'hotty' effect.

- Avocados are higher in fat than other fruits. However, they are excellent sources of vitamin C, folic acid and potassium. So while I encourage you to eat this delectable fruit, do so infrequently, and in smaller quantities than the other fruits.

- Bananas are somewhat drier and therefore can be higher in calories than other fruits. However, they are very good sources of potassium, an electrolyte that is critical for our bodies. Try to eat bananas somewhat less often than other fruits.

Protein The proteins listed earlier are high-water by virtue of their chemical structure and low fat content. They are also 'hotty' as they are complex and require a lot of work in the body to break them down. Furthermore, they do not cause spikes in blood sugar or insulin, so they help to create the proper hormonal effect. Notice that I have not included dried beans and lentils as protein sources appropriate for Phase One. While these are excellent sources of plant-based protein with disease-fighting and 'hotty' properties, they will be introduced in Phase Two, because they can be concentrated sources of calories when overeaten. If you are a vegetarian or vegan, however, you may consider lentils and dried beans as Phase One foods to ensure that you are receiving adequate protein.

TIPS

- When choosing cuts of meat, look for the words 'round' or 'loin' in the name. These varieties, such as striploin, sirloin, tenderloin and eye of round, are usually the lowest in 'water-hating' fat. Fat repels water – i.e., oil and water don't mix, so foods high in fat are often lower in water! Or simply ask the butcher for the lowest-fat cuts. Always trim and discard any visible fat and use low-fat cooking techniques, spices and seasonings that are flavourful yet fat-free, and healthy oils (see right column of the preceding chart).
- Lean sources of red meat are very rich sources of easily absorbable iron. Diets low in iron can lead to low blood levels and feelings of fatigue and low energy.
- Give grass-fed, as opposed to grain-fed, cuts of meat a try. Imagine a high-water food eating a high-water food ... wow!

- Many people are concerned that seafood such as prawns and squid raises blood cholesterol levels. However, these foods are extremely high in omega-3 fatty acids and low in saturated fat. Omega-3 fatty acids have been shown to decrease the risk of heart attack, stroke and inflammation. The cholesterol contained in seafood is therefore offset by their high-water, low-saturated-fat content and disease-fighting properties. In fact, omega-3 fatty acids are so good for us that many cardiologists now recommend taking fish oil supplements!
- When preparing poultry, meat and fish, use modest amounts of healthy fats like olive oil or light cooking spray. Use tomato-based sauces instead of cream or butter sauces. Use herbs and spices to enhance flavour. Use low-fat, water-preserving cooking techniques such as poaching, boiling, steaming and microwaving as often as possible.

Dairy The dairy products listed in the preceding chart contain an excellent healthy combination of protein and carbohydrate. The protein helps slow the absorption of milk sugar into our blood, which helps stabilize insulin levels, thus creating a good hormonal effect. The protein also helps to keep 'hotty' potential high. The low-fat nature of these products ensures that the 'water-hating' fat has been removed, making them less calorific and much better for weight loss.

TIPS

- Dairy products contain calcium, which we need to keep our bones strong and healthy. Osteoporosis (thin, weak bones) affects many individuals at some point in their lives and has a high associated mortality rate, so getting calcium in our diet is very important.
- Studies show that diets high in low-fat dairy products are associated with both weight and fat loss.
- Including fat-free yogurt and milk in our diet (or calcium supplements) can help us beat the bloat. Calcium is exchanged for sodium (salt) in our bodies. So the more calcium we consume, the more salt we should shed. When we shed salt, water goes along with it and, voilà, we're beating the bloat! This is a great trick for premenstrual bloating and has even been shown to decrease menstrual cramps as well!

Drinks The drinks listed earlier are extremely high in water. However, that does not mean that they are all created equal.

TIPS

- When we drink ice-cold water, our bodies must do work to warm the water to body temperature. This requires that the body produces heat ('hotty')! Thus, we actually burn calories when we drink cold water.

- **Note:** While drinking beverages cold may help you burn a few additional calories, please note that if you have digestive troubles, you may want to avoid this, as according to traditional modalities of eating (Indian and Chinese), drinking beverages at room temperature is preferable for digestion.
- Studies have shown that drinking green tea will cause our bodies to burn calories as heat ('hotty'), activate our fat-burning hormones and slow the absorption of sugar into the blood. Drink green tea often to expedite weight loss.
- Green tea inhibits amylase, the enzyme that breaks down carbohydrates, so it can reduce the amount of carbohydrate digested. This allows us to dispose of some of the carbohydrate calories we've ingested! Green tea is also great for curbing cravings for sweet stuff. Try it. The next time you crave a sweet, have a glass of green tea first and see what happens!
- If you add sugar and fat to coffee and tea, you add calories. I used to waste calories by mindlessly adding cream and sugar to my morning coffee. Now I simply add skimmed milk. You'll be amazed at how quickly your palate adapts. The thought of sugar in my coffee now makes me cringe. If you want to jazz up your java, use flavour enhancers like cinnamon, nutmeg, vanilla extract and artificial sweetener.
- Many people confuse the sensations of hunger and thirst. Have you ever eaten platefuls of Chinese food, only to feel hungry an hour or two later? Chinese food can be extremely high in sodium (salt), which is dehydrating. Our bodies may actually be thirsty for water rather than hungry for more food; we just mistake

the sensations, which leads us to overconsume. The next time you feel hungry, have a glass of water first and re-evaluate. Remember, if you drink the water-ice cold, you'll actually burn calories while wondering whether or not you're hungry!

Fats Although I have included fats in Phase One, this category must be approached differently than the others. This is because fat, by virtue of its chemical structure, repels water (oil and water don't mix). However, not all fats are created equal. Monosaturated and polyunsaturated fats, like the ones often found in high-water foods such as fish and vegetables, are very good for our health and have therefore been selected as appropriate for Phase One. While they should not be consumed in excessive quantities, when used in moderation they can help promote weight loss by helping keep us full and slowing the absorption of sugar into our blood. So fats help the body stabilize blood sugar and insulin levels, thus creating a positive hormonal environment. Use the fats listed above to cook and dress foods, but use them sparingly (try for no more than 3 tablespoons per day). Use fat-free cooking sprays and nonstick cookware whenever possible to reduce the amount of added fat.

Low-fat salad dressings and mayonnaises have also been included in this category. Although they are labelled as lower in fat, many of them still contain quite a bit. Moreover, most contain quite a lot of sugar. So when using these dressings, watch your serving size. I recommend not using more than 2–3 tablespoons of salad dressing per salad. I mix 2 tablespoons of low-fat salad dressing with an equal part of vinegar and then dress my salads. Similarly, I often mix 1 tablespoon low-fat mayonnaise with some vinegar when mixing tuna salad. I find this dilution trick quite helpful, as I have been known to consume giant salads, which obviously need more than 2–3 tablespoons of dressing! Use your own judgment, as there are a wide variety of salad dressings available. I will list a few of my favourites later in the book. Stick to dressings that have fewer than 30 calories per tablespoon. Of course, when you have time, it is always best to make your own fresh dressings using ingredients such as the healthy oils listed earlier plus vinegars, herbs and even berries and a sugar substitute if necessary.

TIPS

- Cooking sprays are low enough in calories that you needn't worry about quantity. For the rest of the listed fats, try not to exceed 3 tablespoons per day. Although these are healthy fats that our bodies need, they still contain 9 calories per gram, roughly 120 calories per tablespoon
- Use chicken, vegetable or beef stock or fat-free Italian dressing to 'sauté' foods wherever possible
- Substitute the healthy fats listed above for less healthy fats such as butter wherever possible.

Extras   In addition to being virtually calorie-free, many of the 'extras' permitted in Phase One can actually help increase weight loss through their 'hotty' properties! Use these 'extras' as freely as you like and jump-start weight loss.

TIPS

- It should come as no surprise that hot peppers, such as chilli peppers and cayenne pepper, and hot mustard are 'hotty'! In fact, these foods are such 'hotties' that we feel hot after eating them! If you can handle the spice, go for it. You will burn extra calories when consuming these items.

- Eating ginger can raise our metabolism and help us burn off calories as heat because ginger causes our body temperature to increase. It's 'hotty' indeed! Use fresh ginger in stir-fries, with fish or in a tea.

- Cinnamon is my favourite spice and a dieter's best friend. I mix cinnamon with a low-calorie sweetener or stevia and sprinkle it on oatmeal, fruit and my morning coffee. It's even great on tomato sauce, squash and sweet potatoes. (Note: oatmeal and sweet potatoes will be introduced in Phase Two).

- Soy sauce has a lot of salt, which can cause bloating. Opt for low-sodium varieties whenever possible.

- Stock up on different flavours of vinegars, such as red wine, white wine, apple cider, balsamic, rice wine and fruit. Because vinegar is high in acid and virtually calorie-free, it aids in weight loss! I combine vinegars with a touch of olive oil, herbs, cinnamon and sweetener to make delicious, low-calorie salad dressings.

- Although sugar substitutes are great calorie savers, many people worry that they are harmful. However, here is some information that may ease your mind. Aspartame, a commonly used sugar substitute, is made from protein and is 200 times sweeter than sugar, so a little goes a long way. The UK government has set the acceptable daily intake (ADI – the amount that is considered safe and will not cause harm) as 40 milligrams per kilogram of body weight per day. For the average person, this amounts to about 15 fizzy diet drinks or 181 packets of sweetener per day! Sucralose, better known as Splenda, is another common sugar substitute and is made from sugar, making it more palatable and better suited for baking. The ADI for Splenda is 9 mg/kg/day. For the average person, this is roughly equivalent to 58 packets of Splenda per day! Even so, do try to substitute foods containing sugar substitutes for unprocessed products.

Basic Grocery List To Get You Started

The following is a good grocery list to get you started; read the Phase One ingredients and recipes and pick up any additional ingredients that you need.

Dairy:
Skimmed milk
Artificially sweetened fat-free yogurts and mousses – assorted flavours (Danone and Yeo Valley make great-tasting yogurts)
Reduced-fat feta cheese
Reduced-fat cottage cheese
Reduced-fat soured cream
Reduced-fat ricotta cheese

Condiments, herbs and spices, and dressings and oils:
Cinnamon
Splenda, Canderel (or other sweetener)
Soy sauce
Sesame oil
Olive oil
Cooking spray

Balsamic vinegar
Rice wine vinegar
White wine vinegar
Fat-free mayonnaise

Low-fat salad dressings (Newman's Own are excellent)

Dill
Parsley
Cayenne powder
Ginger – fresh or frozen
Garlic
Olives
Lemon juice

Vegetables
Iceberg lettuce
Romaine lettuce
Mixed bags of assorted lettuce leaves
Cabbage
Red onion
Tomatoes – whole, plum and/or cherry tomatoes
Celery
Carrots – bags of baby carrots are good to have
Spring onions
Green beans
Cucumber
Asparagus (fresh and canned)
Palm hearts (canned – expensive but delicious!)
Spaghetti squash
Broccoli
Cauliflower
Mushrooms (assorted varieties)
Frozen spinach
Frozen bags of mixed vegetables (great for stir-fries)

Fruits
Fresh and/or frozen berries (eg. blueberries, blackberries, raspberries and strawberries)
Apples
Oranges
Grapefruit
Pears
Grapes

Protein
Skinless, boneless chicken breasts
Lean ground chicken and turkey
Assorted fish (eg. salmon, halibut, mackerel)
Low-fat firm tofu
Reduced-fat cooked meat slices (e.g., turkey, ham, chicken)
Soy and whey-based protein powder (choose one that is low-fat and artificially sweetened)
Canned tuna, packed in water

Soups
Vegetable broth/consomme
Miso soup, packaged
Chicken and beef broth/consomme

Desserts
Sugar-free jellies (e.g. Hartleys Sugar Free)
Low-fat artificially sweetened frozen treats such as low-calorie ice cream sticks
Diet hot chocolate (e.g. Highlights)

Beverages
Water
Green tea
Sparkling water (e.g., Perrier)
Diet fizzy drinks
Coffee

PHASE ONE

Appropriate Recipes

Now that you know which foods are suitable for Phase One, let's look at some recipe ideas appropriate for this phase. Some of these recipes will be included in the 14-day sample menu plan to follow.

BREAKFAST

Basic Egg White Omelette

Remember, egg whites are very high in water and easy to prepare, so definitely include them when trying to lose weight.

4 to 5   egg whites, or 120 to 150 g (4 to 5 ½ oz) or low-fat liquid egg substitute (I buy mine in the carton so I don't have to fuss with cracking eggs and discarding yolks)
Cooking spray
Salt and freshly ground black pepper
23-cm (9-inch) microwave-safe dish with a cover

Spray dish with cooking spray. Pour in as much egg white as you want. Sprinkle with salt and pepper. Cover. Microwave on high for about 3 minutes (cooking times may vary depending on your microwave's power).

A perfect omelette – better and easier to clean up than one made in a frying pan! This method is a real time-saver in the morning, as you can dress and get organised while your breakfast is cooking.

If you want to add cheese, cook the eggs as above. Remove cover, add cheese (use feta in Phase One; other low-fat cheeses will be introduced in Phase Two), cover and let sit for a minute or so until cheese melts.

This is the basic recipe; you can add other ingredients to the egg whites before microwaving. Experiment with different vegetables, putting them in the covered dish with the egg whites – the vegetables will steam as the omelette cooks. Here are some of my favourites to help you get started.

Options

Asparagus, Feta and Olives Chop fresh asparagus stems and tips, discarding the woody bottoms. Add to the egg whites, cover and microwave. Remove lid, add feta cheese and sliced olives, cover and leave to sit for a minute to melt the cheese and heat the olives. Enjoy!

Bacon and Green Onion Cut low-fat precooked bacon (or low-fat chicken or ham bacon) into small pieces. Slice green onion. Add both to egg whites, then microwave for 3 minutes. Perfecto!

Herbs Add fresh herbs like parsley, dill, or basil to the egg whites before microwaving for 3 minutes. Tasty, filling, and very healthy.

Basic Smoothie

This is another delicious and easy-to-make breakfast staple.

1	container (170 g/6 oz) sugar-free fat-free yogurt, any flavour	
75 mL	cold water	2½ fl oz
35 g	fresh or frozen berries	1¼ oz
35 g	low-fat firm tofu	1¼ oz
15 g	Splenda or other sweetener	1 tbsp
	Cinnamon to taste	

Place yogurt, water, berries and tofu in blender. Add Splenda, some sprinkles of cinnamon and blend to desired texture. Add ice if you like.

Don't worry if you don't love tofu. It thickens the smoothie, adds protein and simply takes on the flavour of the fruit and yogurt. Tofu can also be replaced by banana, if desired.

Basic Protein Shake

100 g	fresh or frozen berries	4 oz
55 g	sugar-free protein powder	2 oz
225 mL	cold water	8 fl oz
15 mL	flaxseed oil (optional)	1 tbsp
	Sugar substitute to taste	

Place berries, protein powder, water, oil, and sugar substitute in blender and blend until creamy. Add ice and enjoy!

Lunch and Dinner

Salads

Salads can be mixed to taste – add more of one ingredient that you like and less of another that you don't.

Basic Tuna Salad

> White wine vinegar
> Fat-free mayonnaise
> Can (185 g/6½ oz) tuna packed in water, drained
> Spring onions, chopped
> Celery, chopped
> Salt and freshly ground black pepper

Add vinegar to mayo and then combine mayonnaise mixture, tuna, spring onions, celery and salt and pepper. Serve with a squeeze of lemon, if you like.

Iceberg Lettuce Wrap

1   head iceberg lettuce

Discard any damaged or discoloured outer leaves. Cut lettuce in half. Carefully peel off outer leaves. Use three layers of leaves per wrap so that it is strong enough to hold a filling. This is an excellent substitute for bread.

Greek Salad

Delicious topped with grilled chicken, chicken or turkey slices, or even canned tuna.

> Iceberg lettuce, chopped
> Red onion, sliced
> Tomatoes, sliced
> Olives, black or Kalamata
> Green pepper, sliced
> Light feta cheese, crumbled

Combine lettuce, red onion, tomatoes, olives, pepper and feta in a bowl.

DRESSING
Use Basic Balsamic Dressing (see recipe, page 103) or any low-fat Greek dressing (diluted with balsamic vinegar).

Note: Greek salad can be an excellent choice at a restaurant, provided that you ask for the dressing on the side. Because restaurants tend to use a lot of feta, which adds taste and texture, I find that balsamic vinegar is all that is needed to dress the salad.

Cobb Salad

> Romaine lettuce, chopped
> Iceberg lettuce, chopped
> Cooked, sliced chicken or turkey
> Hard-cooked egg white
> Back bacon, cooked and crumbled
> Whole tomatoes, chopped, or cherry tomatoes, halved
> Avocado, peeled and sliced (remember, avocados
> are high in fat compared to other fruits, so don't
> overdo it)

Combine lettuces, chicken, egg white, bacon, tomatoes and avocado in a bowl.

DRESSING
Use Sweet Balsamic Dressing or Tangy Mustard Dressing, (see recipes, pages 103 and 105). Shop-bought low-fat honey mustard dressing also works well. Remember to dilute the dressing with a vinegar of your choice.

Warm Asian Chicken Salad

DRESSING

30 mL	sesame oil	2 tbsp
30 mL	rice wine vinegar	2 tbsp
30 mL	low-sodium soy sauce	2 tbsp
30 mL	Splenda or other sugar substitute	2 tbsp

SALAD

Skinless, boneless chicken breasts, sliced
Water chestnuts (these are very high in water, are great
in salads, and add tons of crunch)
Iceberg lettuce, chopped
Baby spinach
Beansprouts
Mangetout
Cucumber, sliced

DRESSING

To make dressing, combine the sesame oil, rice wine vinegar, soy
sauce and Splenda in a small bowl and set aside.

SALAD

Heat frying pan and spray with cooking spray. Add chicken to pan
and sauté. When brown, add in the dressing and the water
chestnuts. Continue to sauté until chicken and water chestnuts are
done. Meanwhile, toss lettuce, spinach, beansprouts, mangetout
and cucumber to make a salad. Pour cooked chicken mixture over
salad and enjoy!

Asian-Style Cucumber

1	Cucumber, peeled and sliced	
15 mL	rice wine vinegar	1 tbsp
10 mL	soy sauce	2 tsp
5 mL	sesame oil	1 tsp
	Sugar substitute to taste	

Combine cucumber, vinegar, soy sauce and sesame oil in a small bowl. Add sugar substitute to taste.

Coleslaw

1	red cabbage, quartered and thinly sliced	
1	red onion, thinly sliced	
75 mL	fat-free sour cream	2½ oz
75 mL	fat-free mayonnaise	2½ oz
15 mL	balsamic vinegar	1 tbsp
15 mL	white wine vinegar	1 tbsp
5 g	dried tarragon	1 tsp
	Sugar substitute to taste	
	salt and freshly ground black pepper to taste	

Mix cabbage, red onion, sour cream, mayonnaise, vinegars, tarragon, sugar substitute and salt and pepper in a large bowl. Refrigerate for at least 6 hours to allow flavours to blend.

Grilled Portobello Mushrooms

Balsamic vinegar
Fat-free Italian dressing
Salt and freshly ground black pepper
Basil
4–5   Portobello mushrooms

Whisk together vinegar, Italian dressing, salt, pepper and basil. Pour over mushrooms.

Line a baking sheet with foil and spray with cooking spray. Place mushrooms on sheet and bake for approximately 20 minutes at 180°c/350°F/Gas 4.

Salad Dressings

Basic Balsamic Dressing

Makes about 250 mL (9 fl oz) of dressing – to make 1 serving, quarter the recipe).

60 mL	olive oil	4 tbsp
60 mL	balsamic vinegar	4 tbsp
1–2	cloves garlic, minced	
	Salt and freshly ground black pepper to taste	
	Fresh or dried basil to taste	

Place oil, vinegar, garlic, salt, pepper and basil in a jar with lid, shake well and refrigerate. Alternatively, you can place in a blender and add berries and sweetener for a delicious sweet version.

Sweet Balsamic Dressing

Makes about 250 mL (9 fl oz) of dressing – to make 1 serving, quarter the recipe)

60 mL	olive oil	4 tbsp
60 mL	balsamic vinegar (or raspberry vinegar)	4 tbsp
60 mL	water	4 tbsp
60 g	Splenda	2¼ oz
60 g	fat-free sugar-free plain yogurt	2¼ oz
	Pinch salt and freshly ground black pepper	

Place oil, vinegar, water, Splenda, yogurt, salt and pepper in a jar with lid. Shake well and refrigerate.

Oriental Dressing

This is also a great sauce to sauté vegetables, chicken and beef.
Makes 1 cup.

15 mL	reduced-sodium soy sauce	1 tbsp
15 mL	sesame oil	1 tbsp
75 mL	rice wine vinegar	5 tbsp
30 g	grated fresh ginger	2 tbsp
1	clove garlic, minced	
5 g	cornflour	1 tsp
	Sugar substitute to taste	

Bring soy sauce, sesame oil, vinegar, ginger, garlic, cornflour and sugar substitute to a boil in a saucepan over medium-high heat. Cook for about 1 minute, until slightly thickened. Cool to room temperature.

Tangy Mustard Dressing

60 mL	white wine vinegar	4 tbsp
40 g	Splenda	3 tbsp
5 mL	olive oil	1 tsp
5 g	Dijon mustard	1 tsp
30 g	fat-free sugar-free plain yogurt	2 tbsp

Whisk together vinegar, Splenda, oil, mustard and yogurt in a small bowl.

Sesame Dressing

30 mL	chicken stock	2 tbsp
22 mL	rice or white wine vinegar	1½ tbsp
22 mL	soy sauce	1½ tbsp
15 mL	sesame oil	1 tbsp
	Splenda to taste	

Whisk together stock, vinegar, soy sauce, sesame oil and Splenda in a small bowl.

Soups

Breakthrough Mushroom Soup

This recipe is fantastic! It makes a large pot of soup that is delicious, filling and so good for you. You can freeze portions for when you don't feel like cooking.

3	packets (15 g/½ oz each) dried mushrooms	
30 mL	olive oil	2 tbsp
	Cooking spray	
1	onion	
1 L	chicken stock	1¾ pints
700 g	fresh mushrooms, sliced (shiitakes taste best, but regular button mushrooms can be used to reduce cost)	1 lb 9 oz
60 mL	skimmed (semi if you like it creamier) milk	4 tbsp
60 mL	dry sherry	4 tbsp
	Salt and freshly ground black pepper to taste	

Boil 750 mL (1¼ pints) of water and remove from heat. Soak dried mushrooms in the hot water for 30 minutes.

Meanwhile, in a large saucepan, heat olive oil and sauté chopped onion for 5–7 minutes, until golden. Add fresh mushrooms and cook for 3 minutes.

Strain the soaked mushrooms over a bowl and reserve the liquid. Add 500 mL (18 fl oz) of this drained liquid along with the chicken stock to the saucepan. Stir in the drained mushrooms. Simmer for 20 minutes. Remove from heat.

Transfer the mixture to a blender or food processor and purée in batches. Pour the puréed soup back into the saucepan. Add a quarter of the milk, a quarter of the sherry and salt and pepper to taste. Cook for another 3 minutes.

You can eat the soup right away or freeze for later use. Enjoy. You will love this recipe!

The Best Homemade Chicken Soup

This takes some time to make, but it's worth it! You'll have tons to refrigerate and freeze for later use. Great for a quick, healthy meal!

1	chicken, 1.3–1.8 kg (3–4 lbs), cut up into 8 or 9 pieces	
15 g	salt, or more to taste	1 tbsp
	freshly ground black pepper	
1	bunch fresh parsley	
1	bunch fresh dill	
1	bunch celery	
700–900 g	carrots (about 10 medium)	1½–2 lbs
700–900 g	onions (about 5 medium)	1½–2 lbs
2–3	parsnips (skip these in Phase One but add them in Phase Two)	
	Salt and freshly ground pepper	

Put chicken in the bottom of a large pot, cover with water and add salt. The pot should be less than two-thirds full. Bring to a full boil over high heat. Skim off any foam and discard.

Add the pepper, parsley, dill, and celery heart, leaves and a few stalks.

Cut one-quarter of the carrots and onions (and 1 parsnip, if using) into chunks. Add to the pot.

Simmer for 3 hours, adding water as necessary to keep the pot two-thirds full. If you have a fat skimmer, repeatedly skim off the fat that comes to the top.

Remove from heat; strain out chicken and vegetables. If you didn't skim off the fat, you'll have to leave the soup in the refrigerator to chill (probably overnight), until the fat on top solidifies. It can then be lifted off easily.

Dice remaining celery, carrots and parsnips (if using).

Return soup to a boil, add chopped vegetables and simmer for about ½ an hour more. Meanwhile, remove chicken from bones, chop the meat and return to soup. (The vegetables used in making the stock can be eaten as is or chopped and added back to soup.)

Add salt and pepper to taste.

Fish and Meat Dishes

Basic Fish

Spray microwave-safe dish with cooking spray and lay fish (cod, tilapia, halibut, sole or salmon, frozen or fresh) on bottom. Sprinkle fish with salt, pepper, fresh or dried (either-or, although fresh is always better) dill and freshly squeezed lemon. Cover dish with plastic wrap, leaving a corner open for steam to escape. Microwave on high for 3–5 minutes, until fish flakes. That's it! Nothing could be easier. I find that fish cooks best in the microwave – and it's so quick and easy to do. Experiment with different sauces, marinades and spices to add flavour. You can also add vegetables – such as broccoli, onions, peppers, asparagus, cucumbers, etc., to the fish before microwaving. They steam perfectly and infuse the fish with flavours. An entire meal in just a few minutes!

Tilapia Pockets

Makes 4 servings.

30 mL	balsamic vinegar	2 tbsp
60 mL	Newman's Own Light Thai Sesame Dressing (or another light marinade)	4 tbsp
4	tilapia* fillets, cut into 1-cm (½-inch) strips	
1	can water chestnuts, drained	
1	bunch asparagus, woody ends trimmed	
1	onion, sliced	
1	green pepper, sliced	
	Salt and freshly ground black pepper	

Mix the vinegar and Thai Sesame Dressing. Marinate the fish and vegetables in the mixture for about 30 minutes.

Preheat the oven to 230°C/450°F/Gas 8.

Tear aluminum foil into 20- × 30-cm (8- × 12-inch) squares. Spray the squares with cooking spray. Arrange fish, water chestnuts, asparagus, onion and green peppers in centre of foil. Season with salt and pepper to taste. Fold sides to form a sealed packet. Place in oven directly on rack and bake for 15–25 minutes, depending on desired crunch of vegetables.

* You can use any type of fish you like; cod, halibut and salmon would all work. Just experiment. If you don't like fish, you can use skinless, boneless chicken breast, halved and cut into 1-cm (½-inch) strips instead.

Tangy Tilapia
Makes 4 servings.

15 mL	olive oil	1 tbsp
1	small onion, diced	
3	cloves garlic, minced	
2	cans 400 g (14 oz) chopped tomatoes with juice	
125 mL	dry white wine	4 fl oz
	Salt and freshly ground black pepper to taste	
	fresh or dried oregano to taste	
	fresh or dried basil to taste	
4	tilapia fillets cut into bite-size pieces (add scallops, shrimp and/or substitute other white fish as you like)	
55 g	light feta cheese	2 oz

Heat oil in frying pan over medium heat. Sauté onion for a few minutes, until softened, then add garlic and cook for about another 1 minute. Add tomatoes, wine, salt, pepper, oregano and basil and cook for 8–10 minutes longer, until the sauce starts to thicken. Add additional herbs to taste. Add tilapia and cook for about 4 minutes. Sprinkle with feta and serve.

Poached Salmon

Makes 2 servings.

1	romaine lettuce	
2	salmon fillets 115–175 g (4–6 oz each), skin removed	
	Salt and freshly ground black pepper	
15 g	fresh dill (or 5 g/1 tsp dried)	1 tbsp
15 mL	freshly squeezed lemon juice	1 tbsp

Wash and dry lettuce and arrange half the leaves on bottom of microwave-safe rectangular dish. Place salmon on top. Season with salt, pepper, dill and lemon juice. Cover with another layer of lettuce leaves. Microwave for approximately 5 minutes – salmon will flake when ready.

Ginger Salmon

Makes 2 servings.

45 mL	low-sodium soy sauce	3 tbsp
30 mL	sesame oil	2 tbsp
15 g		Splenda
1 tbsp		
60 mL	dry sherry	4 tbsp
3	spring onions, finely chopped	
5 g	freshly grated ginger	1 tsp
2	cloves garlic, minced	
2	salmon fillets (115–170 g/4–6 oz each)	

Combine soy sauce, sesame oil, Splenda, sherry, spring onions, ginger, and garlic in a small bowl.

Spray microwave-safe dish with cooking spray. Place salmon in dish and pour marinade over. Partially cover so that steam can vent. Microwave on high for about 5 minutes, until salmon flakes. Do not eat salmon skin because it contains too much fat.

Tuna Steaks

Makes 2 servings.

40 mL	balsamic vinegar	2–4 tbsp
40 mL	olive oil	2–4 tbsp
2	tuna steaks	
	Steak seasoning	
6	fresh rosemary sprigs, chopped	

Preheat oven to 200°C/400°F/Gas 6 .

Whisk balsamic vinegar and olive oil together.

Place tuna steaks in an ovenproof dish and pour marinade over. Sprinkle with steak seasoning (or salt and pepper) and rosemary.

Cook at for 3–6 minutes per side.

Tofu Delight

Use as much or as little tofu as you like, depending on how much you want to make up for your fridge.

Press a block of extra-firm tofu between paper towels to absorb some of the moisture. Cut into 2.5-cm (1-inch) cubes. Place tofu cubes in a plastic container and pour in Sesame Dressing (see recipe, page 105) to taste. Refrigerate and eat cold as a snack, or sauté cubes in a frying pan, using cooking spray. Tofu Delight is also excellent as a topping for salads or in stir-fries.

'Hotty' Pork Tenderloin

450–900 g	pork tenderloin	1–2 lb
30 mL	sesame oil	2 tbsp
45 g	Splenda or other sugar subsitute	3 tbsp
30 mL	soy sauce	2 tbsp
500 mL	chicken stock	18 fl oz
45 g	grated fresh ginger	3 tbsp
3	cloves garlic, minced	

Place pork, sesame oil, Splenda, soy sauce, chicken stock, ginger and garlic in a large bowl and marinate for at least a few hours, but preferably overnight. Drain and discard marinade.

Preheat oven to 160°C/325°F/Gas 3.

Spray a foil-lined baking sheet with cooking spray. Arrange pork on prepared baking sheet and bake in preheated oven for 25 minutes approximately per 225g/1lb.

'Hotty' Lamb Chops

450 g	lean lamb chops	1 lb
30 mL	water	2 tbsp
15 g	ground cinnamon	1 tbsp
15 g	dry mustard	1 tbsp
	Salt and freshly ground black pepper	

Preheat oven to 180°C/350°F/Gas 4.

Line a baking sheet with foil and spray with cooking spray.

Brush lamb with water and rub with cinnamon, mustard, salt and pepper.

Place lamb chops on prepared baking sheet and cook in preheated oven for approximately 20–30 minutes.

Moroccan Lamb

Makes 4–6 servings.

1	leg of lamb (1.8–2.25 kg/4–5 lbs)	
½	bunch fresh parsley	
½	bunch fresh coriander	
10	cloves garlic	
125 mL	olive oil	4 fl oz
30 g	Dijon mustard	2 tbsp
30 g	ground cumin	2 tbsp
	Salt and freshly ground black pepper	

Trim any fat from the lamb and put the lamb in an ovenproof dish.

Cut slits throughout the lamb 1 cm (½ inch) deep and leave to it sit while you are preparing the other ingredients.

In the meantime, grind the parsley, coriander and garlic in a food processor or blender. Combine with the oil, mustard, cumin, salt and pepper to make a paste.

Preheat oven to 180°C/350°F/Gas 4.

Fill the slits in the lamb with the paste and rub the rest over the lamb. Cover with foil and cook in the preheated oven for 45 minutes. Remove the foil and roast for another 15 minutes to allow the lamb to get crisp.

Side Dishes

Mashed Cauli (You won't believe it's not mashed potatoes)

1	medium head cauliflower	
15 mL	fat-free soured cream	1 tbsp
3 g	minced garlic	½ tsp
0.5 g	chicken soup base or bouillon powder (or ½ tsp salt)	⅛ tsp
	Pinch freshly ground black pepper	
	light cooking spray	

Break cauliflower into small pieces. Cook in boiling water for about 6 minutes, or until soft. Drain well and quickly pat cauliflower dry between several layers of kitchen paper.

In a blender or food processor, purée the hot cauliflower with the soured cream, garlic, chicken soup base and pepper until almost smooth. Serve hot with salt, pepper and light margarine to taste.

Basic Spaghetti Squash

1   spaghetti squash, halved lengthways and deseeded

Preheat oven to 190°C/375°F/Gas 5.

Line a baking sheet with foil and spray with cooking spray. Place squash cut side down on prepared baking sheet and bake for 30 minutes in preheated oven.

Remove from oven and leave to cool until manageable. Take a fork and scrape out pulp, making spaghetti-like strands.

OPTIONS
Below are some great ways to dress your spaghetti squash; I'll give you more options in Phase Two.

Simple Squash

Add salt, pepper and light cooking spray.

Faux Tomato Pasta Primavera

Add tomato sauce and vegetables for a faux tomato pasta primavera.

Cinnamon Squash

Add garlic, cinnamon, sugar substitute and olive oil for a deliciously sweet treat.

Skinny Jicama

Jicama is a root vegetable originally from Central America. You can substitute with carrot or parsnip.

10 mL	rapeseed oil	2 tsp
350 g	jicama, peeled and julienned	12 oz
1	clove garlic, minced	
1	red pepper, cut into thin strips	
0.5 g	sweet or hot paprika	⅛ tsp
0.5 g	salt	⅛ tsp
0.5 g	freshly ground black pepper	⅛ tsp
0.5 g	fresh or dried basil	⅛ tsp

Heat oil in medium frying pan over medium heat. Add jicama, garlic and red pepper. Add seasonings and sauté for about 5 minutes.

Steamed Vegetables

I find that the easiest way to steam vegetables is in the microwave. Use a microwave-safe casserole dish (get a few different sizes, as they come in so handy). Place vegetables (asparagus, green beans, broccoli and cauliflower work well) in dish with a little water, salt and pepper. Cover and microwave on high for about 3–5 minutes. Drain water and add spices, freshly squeezed lemon juice, olive oil or non-hydrogenated light spread to taste.

Try adding garlic and a little light spread or olive oil to the water before microwaving to infuse the vegetables with flavour.

Roasted Vegetables

Preheat oven to 230°C/450°F /Gas 8.

Line a baking sheet with foil and spray with cooking spray.

Toss vegetables (onions, portobello mushrooms, asparagus, broccoli, cauliflower, etc.) in a marinade of your choice. I like to use low-fat Italian dressing with a little salt, peppe, and basil because it's so easy. You can also use balsamic vinegar with a touch of olive oil, salt, pepper, basil and garlic, or soy sauce, rice wine vinegar and sesame oil for an Asian twist.

Scatter vegetables on baking sheet and bake in preheated oven for approximately 30 minutes.

Desserts

Fruit Sorbet

Makes 1 serving.

125 g	frozen berries, partially thawed	4½ oz
15 mL	lemon juice	1 tbsp
	Sugar substitute (such as Splenda or stevia) to taste	

Mix all ingredients in blender or food processor and enjoy immediately. You can also add fat-free, artificially sweetened yogurt for more creaminess. Or try adding a little sparkling water to the blender for a really cool and delicious treat.

PHASE ONE

14-Day Sample Menu Plan

- This is a sample plan. Follow it if you like, or simply use it as a guide.
- Drink water with meals as often as possible.
- Items in italics indicate that a recipe is provided in the preceding section.
- Remember all foods are Phase One–appropriate, so 'yogurt', for instance, means fat-free and artificially sweetened.
- Never eat salad before a meal; always eat it with the main dish. It takes up room on the plate and prevents you from overeating higher-calorie side dishes.

Day 1

BREAKFAST
Coffee with skim milk
Basic Egg White Omelette with asparagus and mushrooms

SNACK
Green tea
Nectarine

LUNCH
Reduced-fat cooked sliced turkey or turkey ham (about 90 g/3¼ oz) on top of mixed salad greens with vegetables of your choice, dressed with low-fat Italian dressing

SNACK
Carrot and celery sticks with low-fat ranch or salsa dip

DINNER
Small green salad, dressed with low-fat dressing of your choice
Tilapia Pockets
Green tea

SNACK
Yogurt

Day 2

BREAKFAST
Coffee with skimmed milk
Basic Smoothie

SNACK
Hard-cooked egg whites and tomatoes

LUNCH
Basic Tuna Salad, on its own or on top of a mixed green salad with fat-free Italian dressing
Apple
Green tea

SNACK
Breakthrough Mushroom Soup

DINNER
Asian-Style Cucumber
'Hotty' Lamb Chops
Steamed Vegetables

SNACK
Sugar-free jelly

Day 3

BREAKFAST
Coffee with skimmed milk
Fat-free cottage cheese, mixed
with berries and sweetened
with Splenda or other sugar
substitute

SNACK
2 tangerines

LUNCH
Cobb Salad
Green tea

SNACK
Basic Smoothie

DINNER
Cherry tomatoes with chopped
green pepper and cucumber,
dressed with *Basic Balsamic
Dressing*
Basic Fish with grilled veg

SNACK
Grapefruit, sweetened with
Splenda mixed with cinnamon

Day 4

BREAKFAST
Coffee with skimmed milk
Basic Protein Shake

SNACK
Plum
Green tea

LUNCH
Reduced-fat cooked meat slices
(about 90 g/3¼ oz) dipped in
hot mustard
Carrots and celery sticks
Yogurt

SNACK
Breakthrough Mushroom Soup

DINNER
Warm Asian Chicken Salad
Low-fat ice cream stick such as
Mini Milk or Skinny Cow
Chocolate Fudge

SNACK
Frozen grapes

Day 5

BREAKFAST
Coffee with skimmed milk
Basic Egg White Omelette with
Asparagus, Feta and Olives

SNACK
Yogurt
Green tea

LUNCH
The Best Homemade Chicken
Soup
Apple

SNACK
Sugarsnap peas and carrots

DINNER
Ginger Salmon
Skinny Jicama
Steamed asparagus

SNACK
Fruit Sorbet

Day 6

BREAKFAST
Coffee with skimmed milk
Reduced-fat cooked ham
– 3 slices
Basic Egg White Omelette
Honeydew and cantaloupe
slices

SNACK
Green tea

LUNCH
Greek Salad

SNACK
Yogurt

DINNER
Lean cut of steak, grilled or
barbecued
Mashed Cauli
Steamed Vegetables

SNACK
Grapefruit, with Splenda mixed
with cinnamon

Day 7

BREAKFAST
Skimmed milk latte
Smoked salmon with sliced
onion, tomatoes and cucumber

SNACK
Fresh fruit salad

LUNCH
Cobb Salad

SNACK
Yogurt

DINNER
Mixed green salad with light
dressing
Faux Tomato Pasta Primavera
with chicken (sauté chicken
with the tomato sauce and
vegetables). Because spaghetti
squash is one of the more
calorific Phase One foods, I
recommend limiting yourself to
about 115 g (4 oz) per serving

SNACK
Pear

Day 8

BREAKFAST
Coffee with skimmed milk
Basic Protein Shake

SNACK
Reduced-fat cottage cheese and
berries, sweetened with Splenda

LUNCH
Greek Salad with grilled chicken

SNACK
Apple
Green tea

DINNER
Poached Salmon
Roasted Vegetables
Asian-Style Cucumber

SNACK
Low-fat ice-cream stick such as
Mini Milk or Skinny Cow
Chocolate Fudge

Day 9

BREAKFAST
Coffee with skimmed milk
Basic Egg White Omelette with herbs

SNACK
Pear
Green Tea

LUNCH
Basic Tuna Salad in *Iceberg Lettuce Wrap*
Tangerine

SNACK
Veggies with low-fat dip

DINNER
Boneless, skinless chicken breast, sautéed or baked, spiced as you prefer
Cinnamon Squash Because spaghetti squash is one of the more calorific Phase One foods, limit yourself to about 115 g (4 oz) per serving
Steamed Asparagus

SNACK
Sugar-free jelly

Day 10

BREAKFAST
Coffee with skimmed milk
Basic Smoothie

SNACK
Green tea
Fresh fruit salad

LUNCH
Cooked slices of turkey, chicken or ham on top of mixed green salad with vegetables and light dressing of your choice
Low-cal hot chocolate

SNACK
Tofu Delight

DINNER
Breakthrough Mushroom Soup
Basic Fish
Steamed green beans

SNACK
Grapefruit, topped with Splenda mixed with cinnamon

Day 11

BREAKFAST
Coffee with skimmed milk
*Basic Egg White Omelette with
Asparagus, Feta and Olives*

SNACK
Apple
Green tea

LUNCH
Faux Tomato Pasta Primavera
Because spaghetti squash is one
of the more calorific Phase One
foods, I recommend limiting
yourself to about 115 g (4 oz)
per serving

SNACK
3 hard-cooked egg whites, with
sliced tomatoes, salt and pepper

DINNER
Tuna Steaks
Coleslaw
Grilled Portobello Mushrooms

SNACK
Frozen grapes
Low-fat ice cream stick such as
Skinny Cow Chocolate Fudge

Day 12

BREAKFAST
Coffee with skimmed milk
Basic Protein Shake

SNACK
Apple
Green tea

LUNCH
Poached Salmon
Mixed green salad

SNACK
Reduced-fat cottage cheese and
berries, sweetened with Splenda

DINNER
'Hotty' Pork Tenderloin
Mashed Cauli
Green salad

SNACK
Yogurt

Day 13

BREAKFAST
Coffee with skimmed milk
*Basic Egg White Omelette with
Bacon and Green Onion*

SNACK
Nectarine
Green tea

LUNCH
Cobb Salad

SNACK
Yogurt

DINNER
Tangy Tilapia
Mixed green salad

SNACK
Fruit Sorbet

Day 14

BREAKFAST
Coffee with skimmed milk
2 low-fat sausages, baked in oven
Basic Egg White Omelette
Watermelon

SNACK
Green tea

LUNCH
Breakthrough Mushroom Soup
Fruit salad with cottage cheese

SNACK
Celery and carrot sticks

DINNER
Basic Fish
Cinnamon Squash Because
spaghetti squash is one of the
more calorific Phase One foods,
I recommend limiting yourself
to about 115 g (4 oz) per serving.
Spinach sautéed in olive oil
with garlic, salt, pepper and
onions

SNACK
Frozen grapes
Sugar-free ice cream stick

A Wider Selection

After two weeks in Phase One, switch to this phase of the diet. Like Phase One, this phase will last two weeks. In this phase, more carbohydrates, such as whole-grain breads, cereals, beans and legumes, are introduced. Also, you can now choose from a wider selection of cheeses, meats and sauces. While the foods introduced in this phase are lower in the 'fourth macronutrient', they still possess the proper 'hotty' and hormonal effects. This means that, despite the lower water content, weight loss will continue, as metabolism and fat-loss hormones remain elevated. While you should still use Phase One foods to form the basis of your diet, you can now add up to three portions of Phase Two foods per day. No more than three portions per day though! Remember, these foods are lower in water, so the calories can quickly add up if you overdo it.

Starting on page 137 you will find a list of foods for you to enjoy now that you are in Phase Two. I have provided information on serving sizes so that you know what constitutes a single portion. As in Phase One, I then discuss each of the categories of foods individually, highlighting their various health benefits. I also offer tips on how to best use and buy these foods as well as on how to estimate portion sizes without having to rely on weights and measures (I mean, get serious!).

Following this information, you will find an extensive collection of Phase Two-appropriate recipes and a 14-day sample menu plan. Once again, you can either follow the plan exactly or simply refer to it for meal ideas.

Foods to Enjoy in Phase Two

While I don't want you weighing and measuring your foods for life, it is important to get a mental picture of what a single portion size looks like. So go get a measuring jug, scales, bowl, tablespoon and plate out of your cupboard. If you have a deck of cards and some dice handy, grab those as well. As you read which foods are appropriate for Phase Two and what constitutes a single portion of that food, measure that food item. Look carefully at how much a single portion size actually amounts to on your plate or in your bowl. *It is absolutely crucial that you do this experiment.* When I first learned this information, I actually used a measuring cup to serve the portion on to my plate or into my bowl. Please trust me – this small effort will benefit your waistline and health for life!

Food	A Portion Is
Bread – must have 100 percent stone-ground, wholemeal, wholewheat, bran, oat hull fibre, oat bran or rye as ingredients. **Those with the terms 'enriched white flour', 'honey', or 'treacle' on the ingredients list cannot be consumed.** (see p. 140)	Bread – 1 slice Pitta – ½ pitta Tortilla – 1 small, ½ large Crispbreads/crackers – 4
Cereal – Porridge (large-flake, slow-cooking whole or rolled oats, as opposed to the instant variety), All-Bran, bran flakes, high-fibre bran	Oats – 90 g (3 oz) dry Bran – 40 g (1½ oz)
Starch – barley; wholewheat pasta; long-grain basmati or wild rice	200 g (7 oz) cooked
Starchy vegetables – Sweet potato and yam; sweetcorn; turnip; parsnip; low-fat/ microwavable or air-popped popcorn	Sweet potato or yam – ½ medium to large Corn – 115 g (4½ oz) canned or 1 cob Turnip – 1 Parsnip – 1 medium Popcorn – 85 g (3 oz) popped

Food	A Portion Is
Dried beans and lentils – soybeans, chickpeas, lentils, butter beans, broad beans, black beans, pinto beans; hummus	40 g (1½ oz) canned or cooked 2 tbsp (30 g) hummus
Nuts and seeds	Nuts – 1 small handful, or about 8 nuts Seeds – 1 tablespoon (15 g)
Animal-source protein – This category includes all meat and egg products that didn't qualify as appropriate for Phase One. These protein sources are higher in fat, which means that they are usually lower in water.	Red meats not listed in Phase One – 85 g (3 oz) hamburger – 85 g (3 oz). This is roughly the size of 2 McDonald's regular hamburger patties or ½ a typical restaurant patty Dark meat of chicken or turkey – 85 g (3 oz) Duck – 85 g (3 oz) Fatty cooked meat slices – 85 g (3 oz) (those not listed in Phase One) Bacon – 2 strips Sausage – 2 small or 1 large Weiner – 1 Meatballs – 85 g (3 oz); 2 large or 4 small Egg with yolk – 2

Food	A Portion Is
Dairy – goat cheese and cream cheese; any hard cheeses; chocolate milk (continue to choose reduced-fat varieties of all dairy products to maximise weight loss)	Goat cheese and cream cheese – 2 tbsp (30 g) Solid cheese – 1 oz (30 g) Skimmed or semi-skimmed chocolate milk – (250 mL/9 fl oz)
Fats – All oils that didn't qualify as appropriate for Phase One, (including full-fat salad dressings, butter, margarine, mayonnaise)	1 tbsp (15 mL)
Extra – any condiments or sauces that weren't listed in Phase One	See page 144

Carbohydrates

This category includes the breads, cereals, and starches listed in 'Foods to Enjoy in Phase Two'.

TIPS

- To avoid unwanted added sugar, always buy oatmeal plain and flavour it yourself. I like to add cinnamon mixed with sugar substitute, berries (fresh or thawed), and some flaked almonds. Try it cold with skimmed milk; it's a wonderful alternative to prepared cereals.
- Always buy large-flake, slow-cooked oats and not the 'instant' or 'quick-cooking oats' variety. Instant varieties have been altered to make them less 'hotty', so we burn fewer calories when we digest them.
- Oatmeal and barley are extremely high in soluble fibre and are therefore 'hotty', helping stabilise blood sugar and insulin levels. Diets high in soluble fibre help prevent diabetes and high cholesterol, two of the biggest risk factors for strokes and heart attack. Remember, a bowl of oatmeal or barley a day helps keep the cardiologist away!
- Do not buy breads, pittas, cereals and crispbreads that have the terms 'sugar', 'enriched white flour', 'honey', or 'molasses' in the ingredient lists. These are not 'hotty'. Most often, the shorter the list of ingredients, the better!
- The coarser the bread or crispbread, the more insoluble fibre it contains and the more our bodies have to work to break it down. In this way we can dispose of many calories unused. These items are 'hotty' and lead to more stable insulin levels. If you are not used to eating foods

high in insoluble fibre, start slowly with these foods to allow your gut time to adjust to the increased bulk.

- Diets high in insoluble fibre help fight constipation, diverticulitis and colon cancer. Remember to drink plenty of water with high-fibre foods to ensure regularity.

Starchy Vegetables

These vegetables are higher in carbohydrate content and lower in water than those listed in Phase One. However, they are excellent sources of fibre and nutrients. I frequently choose from this category when selecting my Phase Two food choices for the day.

TIPS

- Eat the skin with your sweet potato and yams. The skin has loads of fibre that will slow the digestion and absorption of the sugar contained within the potato.
- Top sweet potatoes with some cinnamon mixed with Splenda or stevia for a deliciously sweet and healthy treat.
- Corn is wonderful eaten alone or sprinkled into salads. Do not buy creamed varieties or those with added sugar.
- Popcorn is an excellent snack as it is high in water-loving fibre. In the mood for a sweet snack? Pop some popcorn and then lightly drizzle it with liquid honey, just enough to get it a little sticky. Then sprinkle it with cinnamon, Splenda, some almonds or pecan halves, and bake it in the oven for a few minutes. Voila – candy corn that is 'hotty' and won't spike insulin levels!

Plant-Source Protein

This category includes dried beans and lentils as well as nuts and seeds.

> ### TIPS
>
> - Dried beans and lentils are exceptionally good sources of soluble fibre. These foods are very filling as they attract water in our stomachs and form gels. Therefore, a 125 g (4½oz) serving is very filling. The soluble fibre contained within dried beans and lentils has been shown to help lower cholesterol. Sprinkle them into pasta sauces and salads or use them to make deliciously filling and healthy soups! Always rinse canned varieties with cold water to remove excess salt.
> - Nuts and seeds are excellent sources of protein and fibere. However, they are high in 'water-hating' fat and low in water, so they can be high in calories. If you stick to the recommended portions, you can reap the tasty benefits without packing on pounds.
> - I give nuts and seeds a guest appearance rather than a starring role in my meals. For instance, I add a small handful of toasted pine nuts to salads, a small handful of falked almonds to green beans, 1 tsp (30 mL) of poppy seeds to fish, etc.
> - Nut-based spreads such as peanut butter and Nutella are high in sugar, low in water, high in fat and less 'hotty' than the actual nuts themselves. These items are not appropriate for Phase Two and are best avoided when trying to lose weight.

- Men, eat your pumpkin seeds! An association has been found between pumpkin seeds and protection against prostate cancer.
- Go nuts for almonds. They are an excellent source of disease-fighting fibre and minerals. I buy flaked almonds and toast them in the oven (100°C/400°F/ Gas 6 for 3–5 minutes) on a baking tray. I love to sprinkle them on salads, vegetables, oatmeal and fruit.

Animal-Source Protein

Recall that one portion of most meats is 85 g (3 oz). To help visualize this amount, use the following 'card trick'. An 85-g (3-oz) portion of meat is roughly the size and thickness of a deck of playing cards. Put a deck of cards on your plate. Is this your typical serving size? Probably not! If you have a cut of meat that's twice that thickness, two decks of cards stacked, as I often do, just count it as two portions. If it's twice the thickness and takes up a little more room, count it as three portions. If you order a 255 g (8-oz) steak at a restaurant, and eat it all, you've just eaten three portions. Keep a deck of cards on your kitchen table for the first few weeks that you're on the Hershberg Diet. Each time you eat a higher-fat cut of meat, use it to help estimate your portion size.

This card trick works for almost all kinds of meat. Each time you eat dark meat from a chicken or turkey (remember, the white meat is low in fat, so it qualifies for Phase One), consider how many slices you could fit in the deck of cards. Having a hamburger or hot dog? Think about the size of a deck of cards and judge your portion size based on it. Eventually, you'll get to inherently know the correct portion sizes.

All animal-source proteins (meats and whole eggs) are considered appropriate for Phase Two because proteins are 'hotty' (remember, protein requires a lot of work to break down) and do not cause our blood sugar and insulin levels to spike. However, I suggest that you stick to the lower-fat meats introduced in Phase One as often as possible, saving your three portions of Phase Two foods for the other healthier choices listed above, such as nuts, seeds, dried beans and high-fibre carbohydrates. I tend to eat the Phase Two fatty meats only when I am out at a restaurant. I find that the lower-fat Phase One varieties taste just as good and I know that they are certainly better for my health. However, so long as you stick to the rules, you can choose however you like and still lose weight!

There is one last category that I must mention: extras.

Extras

Extras are any condiments or sauces that weren't listed in Phase One, e.g., honey, teriyaki, cranberry sauce, ketchup, relish, BBQ sauce, etc.

I didn't include extras in the list of Phase Two–appropriate foods because it is far too tedious to measure out portions of condiments and sauces. However, you can include any sauce or condiment that you like in Phase Two and you needn't worry about counting them into your three portions of Phase Two foods per day. Remember that most condiments and sauces are high in either sugar and/or fat, but they do add zing to healthy Phase One and Phase Two foods. So simply be mindful of the types and quantity that you are using, and try to use Phase One spices, sauces, condiments and low-fat dressings in their place as often as possible. A good rule of thumb is to not use more than 2 tablespoons (30 mL) of sauces or condiments per meal and to avoid any sauce that looks creamy or, even worse, has the word 'sweet', 'rich' or 'cream' as a part of its name. These sauces can derail even the most committed dieter's efforts.

PHASE TWO

Appropriate Recipes

Now that you are familiar with the various Phase Two-appropriate foods and their respective portion sizes, let's review some delicious and easy-to-make recipes that incorporate these items. Again, a 14-day sample menu plan will follow.

Now that you are in Phase Two, you have a lot more foods to choose from. You can now jazz up some of the recipe ideas introduced in Phase One. For instance, you can add any type of cheese to omelettes (we were limited to feta in Phase One) and nuts and seeds to vegetables and fish, plus you now have many more sauces to choose from. Just remember to have no more than three portions per day of foods introduced in Phase Two.

Breakfast

Mexican Omelette
Makes 1 serving.

Prepare *Basic Egg White Omelette* as in Phase One. When cooked, remove lid and add up to 40 g (1½ oz) black beans and up to 30 g (1 oz) grated light cheddar cheese. Cover for about 1 minute so the steam will warm the dish up and melt the cheese. Remove lid and top with salsa. Delicious!

The Very Best Cereal
Makes 1 serving.

125 g (4½ oz) oats + 15 g (½ oz) All-Bran or bran
            (total = 1 Phase Two portion)
1 small handful (about 30 g/1 oz, or 8 whole nuts)
1 handful flaked almonds (1 Phase Two portion)
            Fresh berries
            Skimmed milk
            Splenda, mixed with cinnamon

Add the oats, fibre cereal, almonds and berries to skimmed milk. Sweeten with Splenda mixed with cinnamon to taste. Eat cold. This counts as two of your servings of Phase Two foods per day, but it's worth it. It's delicious and excellent for your health.

Lunch and Dinner

SALADS

Jicama, Orange and Almond Salad

If Jicama is unavailable, you can use equal quantities of carrot and celery.

Makes 4 servings.

1	jicama (675 g/1½ lb)	
450–675 g	fresh orange sections	(1–1½ lb)
¼ tsp	salt	
1	dash chilli powder	
115 g	flaked almonds (about 4 small handfuls)	4 oz
45 g	chopped fresh coriander	3 tbsp

Peel and slice jicama; slice into 5-cm (2-inch) strips. Toss with the orange sections, salt and chilli powder. Refrigerate.

Preheat oven to 200°C/400°F/Gas 6.

Five minutes before serving, bake flaked almonds on a baking tray in preheated oven for about 3–5 minutes, being careful that they don't burn (30 g/1 oz of flaked almonds equals approximately one Phase Two portion). Scatter almonds over salad and garnish with chopped fresh coriander.

Caesar Salad

Use portions of the following ingredients to taste, but remember that 30 g (1 oz) of cheese equals one Phase Two portion.

SALAD

    Romaine lettuce, chopped
    Cherry tomatoes
    Bacon bits (it is best to use chopped low-fat turkey ham)
    Freshly grated Parmesan cheese

Toss desired amounts of lettuce, tomatoes, bacon bits and cheese in a large bowl.

DRESSING

60 g	fat-free mayonnaise	2¼ oz
60 g	fat-free plain yogurt (or use 120 g/4½ oz of either mayo or yogurt)	2¼ oz
2 tbsp	freshly squeezed lemon juice	30 mL
1 tsp	olive oil	5 mL
1 tsp	white wine vinegar	5 mL
1 tsp	Dijon mustard	5 mL
1 tsp	Worcestershire sauce	5 mL
2	garlic cloves, minced	
55 g	freshly grated Parmesan (optional)	2 oz

Mix mayonnaise, yogurt, lemon juice, oil, vinegar, Worcestershire sauce, garlic, and cheese.

Pour over salad, toss, and enjoy! This is great topped with grilled chicken breast.

(If you don't want to make your own dressing, buy a low-fat Caesar dressing and dilute with white wine vinegar and lemon juice.)

Apple and Walnut Salad

Makes 4 servings.

SALAD

60 mL	apple cider vinegar	2 fl oz
60 g	mixed with cinnamon	
1–2	green apples, cored and sliced	
115 g	walnut halves or pecan halves (approx. one small handful, per plate, which is one Phase Two portion)	4 oz
400 g	mixed spring greens	14 oz
1	cucumber, sliced	
1	red pepper, sliced	
	Cooking spray	
30 mL	Liquid honey	2 tbsp

DRESSING

45 mL	rapeseed oil	3 tbsp
30 mL	fat-free plain yogurt	2 tbsp
115 g	freshly grated Parmesan cheese (30 g/2 tbsp = 15 g/1 oz per person, which is one Phase Two portion)	4 oz

In a small bowl, combine vinegar and Splenda mixed with cinnamon. Pour over apples and leave to soak.

Combine mixed greens, cucumber and red pepper and set aside.

Microwave liquid honey for about 30 seconds. Reserving liquid, drain apples and place on a large plate with the walnuts. Drizzle both with the honey – just to make them sticky – and toss with Splenda mixed with cinnamon.

Preheat oven to 200°C/400°F/Gas 6. Line a baking tray with foil. Spray with cooking spray and scatter walnuts and apples on top. Bake in preheated oven for about 3–5 minutes, watching carefully so they don't burn. Remove from oven and leave to cool.

Meanwhile, add rapeseed oil and yogurt to reserved soaking liquid. Whisk, adding honey to sweeten to taste.

Toss dressing with salad and scatter apples, walnuts and grated Parmesan over.

Better Than Aubergine Parmesan
Makes 8 servings.

30 mL	olive oil	2 tbsp
1	medium aubergine	
175 g	chopped green pepper	6 oz
1	carton (225 g/8 oz) passata	
1 g	dried oregano, crumbled	¼ tsp
3–4	fresh basil leaves (or 1 tsp/5 g dry basil)	
3–4	cloves garlic, minced	
2 g	fine sea salt	½ tsp
1 g	freshly ground black pepper	¼ tsp
55 g	sliced spring onions (include green tops)	2 oz
55 g	sliced olives (canned or fresh), divided	2 oz
225 g	shredded low-fat mozzarella cheese	8 oz

Cut unpeeled aubergine into 1-cm (½-inch) cubes; set aside. Coat a large microwave-safe dish with olive oil. Microwave, uncovered, on high for 30 seconds to heat oil. Add aubergine and green pepper; mix to coat with the oil. Cover loosely with waxed paper. Microwave on high for 4 minutes.

Combine passata with oregano, basil, garlic, salt, pepper, spring onions and half the olives. Stir into aubergine mixture. Mix in three quarters of the cheese. Microwave, uncovered, on high for 8–10 minutes. Sprinkle with remaining olives and cheese.

Leave to stand for 3 to 4 minutes before serving.

Each serving contains one Phase Two portion.

Salmon Patties

Makes 2 servings.

1	can (418 g/14.75 oz) salmon	
2	egg whites	
5 mL	freshly squeezed lemon juice	1 tsp
½	medium onion, chopped	
2 g	freshly ground black pepper	½ tsp
90 g	oats (1 Phase Two serving)	3 oz
30 mL	rapeseed or vegetable oil	2 tbsp

Empty the can of salmon with juice into a large mixing bowl and remove bones. Add egg whites and lemon juice. Stir well and add onion, pepper and oats. (The oats should absorb the moisture, and you may need less than 90 g/3 oz.) Form into 6 patties and set aside.

Heat oil in a nonstick frying pan and cook patties for approximately 4 minutes per side, until outside is browned and centre is no longer cool.

Alternatively, you can bake the patties in the oven to eliminate the need for oil. Preheat oven to 200°C/400°F/Gas 6. Line a baking tray with foil and spray well with cooking spray. Place patties on foil and bake in preheated oven for 10 minutes, flip, and cook for another 10 minutes. They will be brown and warm inside when done.

Six patties equals one Phase Two portion (for the 90 g/3 oz oats). I find that 3 patties is a good portion size, so you only have to count this as half of a Phase Two portion.

OPTIONS

Tuna Patties

Substitute tuna for salmon, using the same recipe and procedure as for *Salmon Patties*.

Meatballs

Substitute lean ground chicken, turkey, or beef in *Salmon Patties*. Instead of forming into patties, form into meatballs. These taste great topped with a sweet tomato sauce. To make a healthy, sweet-tasting tomato sauce, heat a carton of passata and add spices and sweetener to taste.

Baked Fish

Makes 4 servings.

4	115 g/4 oz fish fillets (tilapia, halibut, sole or cod)	
40 g	fresh mushrooms, sliced	1½ oz
1	green pepper, deseeded and cut into 2.5 cm (1-inch) pieces	
1	onion, sliced	
30 mL	chicken stock or water	2 tbsp
225 g	salsa	8 oz
115 g	freshly grated Parmesan	4 oz

Spray a large microwave-safe dish with cooking spray. Layer fish along bottom and add mushrooms, pepper, onion and stock.

Microwave, covered, with a slight opening for steam to vent on high for 5 minutes. Drain juices. Spoon salsa over the vegetables and cook for another minute or so, until salsa is heated. Top with Parmesan.

Count 1 serving (1 piece of fish) as one Phase Two portion (2 tbsp Parmesan = 30 g/1 oz).

Squash Lasagna

Makes approximately 8 servings.

1	large spaghetti squash	
	Shop-bought tomato sauce of your choice	
115 oz	shredded partly-skimmed mozzarella cheese	4 oz
115 g	Freshly grated Parmesan	4 oz
55 g	sliced black olives	2 oz
500 g	sliced mushrooms	2 oz
1	aubergine, sliced thinly	

Make *Basic Spaghetti Squash* (see recipes, page 122) or pierce a few holes in the squash and microwave on high for approximately 15 minutes. Leave it to cool and then cut lengthways, removing seeds. Scrape spaghetti squash with fork to form strands like spaghetti.

Preheat oven to 180°C/350°F/Gas 4. Spray a 23- × 33-cm (9- × 13-inch) (3L) ovenproof dish with cooking spray. Spoon in tomato sauce to lightly cover the bottom of the dish. Layer spaghetti squash over and pat down. Pour in another layer of tomato sauce. Next place a layer of aubergine, then a layer of half the shredded mozzarella cheese. Place another layer of squash on top, and cover with tomato sauce. On top place a layer of mushrooms and a layer of the remaining mozzarella cheese. Sprinkle Parmesan on top. Bake in preheated oven for 30 minutes.

Count 1 serving of lasagna as 1½ Phase Two portions.

Note: You can substitute sautéed extra-lean ground beef for the vegetables (mushrooms, aubergine and olives) if you want to create a meat lasagna.

Barley with Mushrooms

So good for a cold winter day!
Makes 4 servings.

30 mL	oil (vegetable, rapeseed or olive)	2 tbsp
1	medium onion, chopped	
225 g	mushrooms, sliced	8 oz
225 g	barley	8 oz
	Salt and freshly ground black pepper to taste	
600mL	vegetable stock, boiling	1 pint

Preheat oven to 180°C/ 350°F/Gas 4.

Heat oil in a large frying pan. Sauté onion, mushrooms, barley, salt and pepper. Stir frequently until barley is lightly browned. Place in a large casserole dish (about 2 L/3½ pints) and stir in stock.

Cover and bake in preheated oven for approximately 1 hour. (If barley is too firm when all liquid is absorbed add additional 125 mL/4 fl oz) boiling water and bake another 15 minutes.)

Count 125 mL/4 fl oz as 1 serving, which should be counted as one Phase Two portion.

PHASE TWO

14-Day Sample Menu Plan

- This is a sample plan. Follow it if you like, or simply use it as a guide.
- Drink water with meals as often as possible.
- Items in italics indicate that a recipe was listed in Phase One or Two.
- Notice that there are no more than three servings of Phase Two-appropriate foods per day
- Never eat salad before a meal; always eat it with the main dish.

Day 1

BREAKFAST
Coffee with skimmed milk
Mexican Omelette

SNACK
Pear
Green tea

LUNCH
Half a wholemeal pitta, filled
with low-fat sliced cooked
turkey, alfalfa sprouts, sliced
cucumbers and mustard
Yogurt

SNACK
Veggies with fat-free dip

DINNER
Mixed green salad with low-fat
dressing of your choice
Baked Fish

SNACK
Frozen grapes, 1–2 handfuls

Day 2

BREAKFAST
Coffee with skimmed milk
The Very Best Cereal

SNACK
Yogurt

LUNCH
Greek Salad with chicken

SNACK
Apple

DINNER
Skinless, boneless breast of
chicken, baked or sautéed
Steamed asparagus
Apple and Walnut Salad

SNACK
Sugar-free jelly

Day 3

BREAKFAST
Coffee with skimmed milk
Hot oatmeal (Mix 90 g/3 oz
old-fashioned oats with (375
mL/13 fl oz) water; heat in
microwave according to
package directions. Sweeten
with Splenda mixed with
cinnamon.)

SNACK
Fat-free cottage cheese, mixed
with fruit and sweetened with
Splenda

LUNCH
Mixed green salad with 115 g (4
oz) chickpeas and assorted
vegetables of your choice.
Dress with low-fat dressing.
Apple

SNACK
Breakthrough Mushroom Soup

DINNER
Ginger Salmon
Steamed green beans (I like to
bake flaked almonds in the
oven for about 3 minutes and
add them to the beans.
Remember, for each handful of
nuts, count one Phase Two
portion. Top with salt, pepper
and either olive oil or non-
hydrogenated light spread.)

SNACK
Cherries (about 10)
Sugar-free ice cream stick

Day 4

BREAKFAST
Coffee with skimmed milk
Basic Smoothie

SNACK
3 hard-cooked egg whites

LUNCH
Basic Tuna Salad, mixed with
tomatoes, cucumbers and salad
greens
Fresh fruit salad

SNACK
Carrot and celery sticks

DINNER
Caesar Salad
Squash Lasagna

SNACK
Diet hot chocolate

Day 5

BREAKFAST
Coffee and skimmed milk
*Basic Egg White Omelette with
Asparagus, Feta and Olives*

SNACK
Banana

LUNCH
Turkey sandwich (use low-
fatcooked turkey slices and
place between two pieces of
Phase Two-appropriate bread. I
like to add sliced cucumbers,
tomatoes and hot mustard to
mine.)
Orange

SNACK
85 g/3 oz popcorn, with low-fat
butter or spread and sprinkled
with Splenda mixed with
cinnamon

DINNER
Mixed green salad
Tilapia Pockets

SNACK
Sugar-free ice cream stick

Day 6

BREAKFAST
Coffee with skimmed milk
Basic Protein Shake

SNACK
Green tea

LUNCH
Warm Asian Chicken Salad

SNACK
Slices of fresh fruit

DINNER
Basic Fish
Barley with Mushrooms
(125 mL/4 fl oz)
Steamed asparagus

SNACK
Fruit sorbet

Day 7

BREAKFAST
Coffee with skimmed milk
The Very Best Cereal

SNACK
Tangerine

LUNCH
Poached Salmon
Mixed green salad

SNACK
85 g (3 oz) popcorn

DINNER
Greek Salad
"Hotty" Lamb Chops
Portobello mushrooms,
marinated in low-fat Italian
dressing, balsamic vinegar, salt,
pepper and basil and then
sautéed

SNACK
Frozen grapes, 1–2 handfuls

Day 8

BREAKFAST
Coffee with skimmed milk
Basic Egg White Omelette
One piece toast, with fat-free
cream cheese

SNACK
Green tea
Yogurt

LUNCH
Mixed green salad with
vegetables, grilled chicken, 1
tablespoon (15 mL) sunflower
seeds, and light Italian dressing

SNACK
Apple

DINNER
Sliced turkey breast, (125 mL/
4 fl oz) wild rice and steamed
broccoli

SNACK
Sugar-free jelly

Day 9

BREAKFAST
Coffee with skimmed milk
Two 175 g (6 oz) fat-free,
artificially sweetened yogurts

SNACK
A small handful mixed nuts
Orange

LUNCH
*The Best Homemade Chicken
Soup*
Mixed green salad

SNACK
Semi-skimmed chocolate milk

DINNER
Lean steak
Green beans, with toasted
almonds
Coleslaw

SNACK
Frozen grapes, 1–2 handfuls

Day 10

BREAKFAST
Coffee with skimmed milk
The Very Best Cereal

SNACK
Green tea
Plum

LUNCH
Low-fat cooked turkey slices,
dipped in hot mustard
Yogurt
Carrot and celery sticks

SNACK
Breakthrough Mushroom Soup

DINNER
Basic Fish
Moroccan Lamb
Cucumbers and tomatoes,
tossed in a light vinaigrette

SNACK
Nectarine

Day 11

BREAKFAST
Coffee with skimmed milk
Basic Egg White Omelette

SNACK
2 plums

LUNCH
Cobb Salad with chicken

SNACK
Veggies and fat-free dip

DINNER
Caesar salad with grilled
chicken

SNACK
85 g (3 oz) fat-free popcorn

Day 12

BREAKFAST
Coffee with skimmed milk
Basic Protein Shake

SNACK
Green tea
Orange

LUNCH
Half a wholemeal pitta, filled
with *Basic Tuna Salad*, sliced
cucumber and alfalfa sprouts
Yogurt

SNACK
Grapefruit, topped with
Splenda mixed with cinnamon

DINNER
Apple and Walnut Salad
Lean steak
Steamed asparagus

SNACK
Sugar-free jelly

Day 13

BREAKFAST
Coffee with skimmed milk
Cottage cheese, mixed with
fruit

SNACK
Green tea

LUNCH
Mixed green salad
Salmon Patties

SNACK
Veggetables and low-fat dip

DINNER
Caesar salad
Sautéed chicken and vegetables
in tomato sauce, served over
100 g (3½ oz) wholewheat pasta

SNACK
Fruit sorbet

Day 14

BREAKFAST
Coffee with skimmed milk
2 slices reduced-fat cooked ham
Basic Egg White Omelette
Slices of fruit

SNACK
Green tea

LUNCH
Reduced-fat cooked turkey slices on top of a mixed salad with light dressing

SNACK
85 g (3 oz) fat-free popcorn

DINNER
Lean grilled steak
Roasted Vegetables
Mashed Cauli

SNACK
Diet hot chocolate

Congratulations

You've made it to Phase Three – the final phase for weight loss!
You will remain in this phase until you reach your goal weight. You
should be looking and feeling great. You've probably lost a
noticeable amount of weight as well as having improved your
blood chemistry and overall health. You'll be delighted to know
that in this phase you can eat any food you like. That's right! No
food is off-limits.

Phase Three foods are traditionally thought of as bad for
weight loss; they are low in water, burn few calories in their
breakdown and encourage a fat-storing hormonal effect. These
foods consist mainly of 'white foods', like white bread, potatoes,
rice, pasta, fries and bakery products; snack foods such as crisps,
biscuits and cereal bars; and junk food like chocolate bars, sweets,
fizzy drinks, ice cream, etc. The problem is that these are the foods
we love! In this phase you will learn a strategy so that you can

indulge in these delicious items without destroying your weight loss and health goals.

Phase Three Strategy

1. 1,000 Calories a Week

Because Phase Three foods are costly to your diet, you must keep track of how much you eat of them. The easiest way to do this is with the help of the calorie information on nutrition labels.

To be able to eat Phase Three foods while still losing weight, you must restrict yourself to a limit of no more than 1,000 calories per week of them. It's as simple as that. I suggest that you always round off to the nearest multiple of 100. For example, if the nutrition label on a bar of chocolate says one bar equals 320 calories, and you eat the entire bar, that's fine; you must count 300 calories, so now you have 700 calories left for the week. *Remember, you can still eat as many Phase One foods as you like, plus your three portions of Phase Two foods per day.* If you look at the '7-Day sample Menu Plan' that starts on page 177, you'll see just how easy this is to do.

If you absolutely detest counting and can't keep track of the day of the week, don't worry. However, you must develop a system that limits the amount of Phase Three foods you consume. If you don't, you'll gain weight. Maybe you want to choose a 'cheat' day to treat yourself. Maybe you should eat Phase Three foods only on special occasions. I find that for me the best system is that of 1,000 calories a week, but it's up to you. If you find that weight loss slows in Phase Three or that you are being a little too liberal with these foods, just skip back to Phase One for a week or two until you're back on track.

2. Splurging Tips

These tips include strategies we can use to trick our bodies into thinking that we've consumed a healthier, higher-water food than we have. We are trying to improve the water ratio as well as the 'hotty' and hormonal effect of Phase Three foods.

First, we must find a way to increase the water content and calorie-burning potential of the food. If we consume Phase Three foods with a full glass of cold water or green tea, we accomplish this goal quite easily. Recall that in addition to being obviously high in water, cold water and green tea are 'hotty'. When we drink them, our body is encouraged to burn calories.

Our second goal involves finding a way to improve the hormonal effect; we want to slow the absorption of sugar into our blood. Again, this is easily accomplished. We simply have to eat Phase Three foods with or immediately following a Phase One or Phase Two food, which will tend to have more protein, fibre or fat. All three of these substances slow the rate at which we digest and absorb sugar, thus improving the net hormonal effect. Alternatively, you may choose to eat the Phase Three food along with a fish oil or flaxseed oil supplement (limit supplements to two per day). This will achieve the same effect.

Let's review the Phase Three strategy:
1. Any food that was not listed in Phase One or Phase Two is considered a Phase Three food. Most often, these are 'white foods', snack foods, or junk foods.
2. You may eat up to 1,000 calories per week of Phase Three foods. Note the calories per serving size that you are about to eat, round this number to the closest multiple of 100 and keep track of this amount. Most Phase Three foods are processed snack-type foods that come with nutrition labels, so this task is relatively easy to do. For further help, I have provided estimates

of the calorie counts associated with commonly consumed Phase Three foods in the chart that follows. Whenever the nutrition label is available, though, use it instead.

3. You cannot carry over leftover calories to subsequent weeks. If you do not eat your total allowed amount, you will lose weight a little more quickly!

4. Consume foods with a full glass of cold water or green tea. This increases the water content and makes the food more 'hotty'.

5. Consume foods along with or immediately following meals of Phase One or Phase Two foods. If you want to have the food on its own as a snack, simply take one fish oil or flaxseed oil supplement along with the food.

Examples of Foods to Enjoy in Phase Three

(**Note:** Whenever nutrition labels are available, use them instead.)

Food	Serving	Calorie Count
BREADS with ingredients such as enriched white flour, sugar, honey or fine-ground, which don't qualify as appropriate for Phase Two		
Sliced bread	1 piece	100

Food	Serving	Calorie Count
Pitta	1 medium	200
Tortilla wrap	1 large	200
Bagel	1 whole	300
Pancake	1 large or 2 small	200
Waffle	1 large or 3 small	300
Bread roll	1	100
Muffin	1 large or 2 mini	400
Low-fat muffin	1 large	300
Croissant	1	300
Hamburger/hotdog bun	1	200
Cereals (other than those suitable for Phase Two)	55 g/2 oz	200
Crispbreads	4	100
SIDE DISHES		
Baked potato	1	200
Pasta	200 g (7 oz), cooked	200
Rice	250 g (9 oz). cooked	200
Sushi rice	6 maki (sushi) rolls	100

Food	Serving	Calorie Count
Fried rice	250 g (9 oz), cooked	300
Couscous	200 g (7 oz), cooked	200
French fries	¼ plate portion, or about 20 fries	400
SNACKS AND DESSERTS		
Potato crisps	1 snack size bag (35 g)	180
Pretzels	1 snack size bag (2.0 oz/60 g)	200
Cinema popcorn	1 small bag	600
Biscuits	1 large or 2 small	100
Chocolate bar	1	300
Cereal bar	1	200
Doughnut	1	300
Cake, iced	1 piece	400
Fruit Pie	1 piece	400
SWEETS		
Liquorice	2 pieces	100

Food	Serving	Calorie Count
Jelly beans, wine gums, etc.	10 pieces	100
Hard sweets	5 pieces	100
Dried fruit	1 handful	100
COLD DESSERTS		
Regular ice cream	125 g (4½ oz)	300
Low-fat or fat-free ice cream	125 g (4½ oz)	100
Sherbet, sorbet	125 g (4½ oz)	100
Low-fat or fat-free frozen yogurt	125 g (4½ oz)	100
Milkshakes	1 (about 350 ml/ 12 fl oz)	400
DRINKS		
Cola	1 can (350 ml/12 fl oz)	100
Juice	250 mL (9 fl oz)	100

On the following page, I have provided you with a 7-day sample menu plan to show you what a typical week could look like in Phase Three of the diet.

PHASE THREE

7-Day Sample Menu Plan

- *Drink water with meals as often as possible, as we did in the other phases.*

Day 1

BREAKFAST
90 g (3 oz) plain, large-flake oatmeal, topped with Splenda mixed with cinnamon, and blueberries
Coffee with skimmed milk

SNACK
Apple

LUNCH
Turkey sandwich: low-fat (preferably low-sodium) cooked turkey slices on two slices of 100 percent stone-ground wholegrain bread, with tomato, pickle and mustard
Tangerine
Chocolate-coated cereal bar (**200 calories**), consumed with a full 250 mL (9 fl oz) glass of ice water

SNACK
Carrot and celery sticks with fat-free dip

DINNER
Seasoned boneless, skinless chicken breast
Grilled aubergine, peppers and mushrooms, topped with olive oil and balsamic vinegar
Salad topped with olives, cucumbers and tomatoes, sprinkled with feta cheese, with olive oil and balsamic vinegar dressing
Water

SNACK
Grapefruit, topped with Splenda mixed with cinnamon

Day 1 count of Phase Three foods = 200 calories

Day 2

BREAKFAST
Fat-free cottage cheese, topped with fruit

SNACK
Skimmed milk latte with cinnamon

LUNCH
Chicken breast, grilled
Salad of spinach, cucumber, tomatoes, 1 tablespoon (15 g) sunflower seeds, and light Italian dressing
Water

SNACK
Apple

DINNER
100 g (3½ oz) wholewheat pasta, topped with vegetarian sauce made from mushrooms, onions, garlic, tomato sauce, 115 g (4 oz) chickpeas, olive oil and spices
Caesar Salad
Diet fizzy drink

SNACK
Fat-free, artificially sweetened yogurt

Day 2 count of Phase Three foods = 0
Cumulative count of Phase Three foods = 200 calories

Day 3

BREAKFAST
The Very Best Cereal
Coffee with skimmed milk

SNACK
Fat-free, artificially sweetened
yogurt

LUNCH
Tuna Salad in half a whole
wheat pita
Salad of lettuce, beets,
cucumber and tomato, topped
with low-fat Italian dressing

SNACK
Sugarsnap peas and celery
sticks
Green tea

DINNER
Lean steak, with all visible fat
trimmed
Grilled portobello mushrooms,
brushed with olive oil and
balsamic vinegar
Steamed green beans

SNACK
Frozen grapes, 1–2 handfuls

**Day 3 count of Phase Three
foods = 0
Cumulative count of Phase
Three foods = 200 calories**

Day 4

BREAKFAST
Apple
Coffee with skimmed milk

SNACK
Cereal bar (**200 calories**)
Green tea and flaxseed oil
supplement

LUNCH
Half a wholewheat pitta, filled
with 2 tbsp (30 mL) hummus,
alfalfa sprouts, cucumber,
turkey deli meat, and a few
sliced olives
3 small chocolates (**100
calories**)

SNACK
Decaffeinated skimmed milk
latte
Plum

DINNER
Ginger Salmon
Spinach salad with a small
handful of toasted pine nuts
and cherry tomatoes, with low-
fat strawberry or French
dressing

SNACK
Fat-free, artificially sweetened
yogurt

**Day 4 count of Phase Three
foods = 300 calories
Cumulative count of Phase
Three foods = 500 calories**

Day 5

BREAKFAST
Fat-free cottage cheese with honeydew, cantaloupe and a small handful of flaked almonds
Coffee with skimmed milk

SNACK
Banana
Green tea

LUNCH
Cooked chicken slices atop large salad of mixed greens, cucumber, tomato, peppers, broccoli and 1 tablespoon (15 mL) sunflower seeds, with light dressing
Diet iced tea

SNACK
Nectarine

DINNER
(This in an example of something that you could order at a
restaurant.)
Salad with roasted red peppers, mushrooms, and about 2 tablespoons (30 mL) goat cheese (ask for dressing on side and use sparingly; I often ask for balsamic vinegar and use it instead of the oily dressing)
Baked trout in lemon-dill sauce
Asparagus
Steamed spinach instead of the rice that the trout was supposed to be served with (most restaurants will substitute vegetables for other side dishes if you ask)
2 glasses of red wine
½ slice decadent chocolate cake
(400 ÷ 2 = 200 calories)

Day 5 count of Phase Three foods = 200 calories
Cumulative count of Phase Three foods = 700 calories

Day 6

BREAKFAST
Basic Egg White Omelette with mushrooms, spinach, onions, salsa, and 30 g (1 oz) shredded low-fat cheddar cheese
2 slices cooked turkey
Orange
Coffee with skimmed milk

LUNCH
Salad of mixed dark greens with cooked turkey slices, cucumbers, tomatoes, peppers, and 1 tablespoon (15 mL) sunflower seeds
Green tea

DINNER
(If you love sushi, here is an example of how to fit it into your diet.)
Miso soup
Green salad
Salmon sashimi
6 spicy tuna rolls with ginger and light soy sauce – ask to hold mayo in rolls **(100 calories for the sushi rice)**
Orange

SNACK
Sugar-free ice cream stick

Day 6 count of Phase Three foods = 100 calories
Cumulative count of Phase Three foods = 800 calories

Day 7

BREAKFAST
Basic Egg White Omelette with Asparagus, Feta and Olives
Coffee with skimmed milk

LUNCH
The Best Homemade Chicken Soup
Vegetables and fat-free dip

SNACK
Crisps (25 g/1 oz) (**200 calories**), consumed with 1 375 mL (12 fl oz) glass of ice-cold water and flaxseed oil supplement

DINNER
Salad with tomatoes, cucumber, and sautéed wild mushrooms, with olive oil and vinegar dressing
BBQ ribs (4)
BBQ chicken
Steamed green beans with toasted almonds (in moderation)
Roasted red peppers

SNACK
Sugar-free jelly

Day 7 count of Phase Three foods = 200 calories
Cumulative count of Phase Three foods = 1000 calories!

PHASE FOUR

Maintenance

You did it! You look great, and I bet you feel great too. So, how can you prevent the pounds from coming back? It's all about maintenance!

This lifelong maintenance phase is simple; it's virtually the same as Phase Three. The only difference is how you approach the foods introduced in Phase Two. These are the foods that are lower in water than those introduced in Phase One. During Phase Two you limited yourself to no more than three portions per day. But also recall that Phase Two foods are 'hotty' and help to stabilize blood sugar and insulin levels; they are also great for the prevention of many medical conditions and ailments. So now that you have reached your goal weight, I encourage you to indulge in these healthy foods; you no longer have to limit yourself to three servings per day. Just use your weight as your guide. If it starts to climb a little, cut back. Soon enough, you will learn exactly what your body requires to stay healthy, thin and gorgeous!

Acknowledgements

I would like to acknowledge the following people for their help, guidance and support.

To my agent, Rick Broadhead, thank you for your dedication, advice, hard work and steadfast belief in both my project and me personally from the very beginning. Your support and encouragement helped transform my vision into a reality and I am forever grateful.

Thank you to the entire team at Key Porter Books for your willingness to take a chance on a first time author. I am most grateful for your commitment to this project and for the many hours of hard work that were dedicated to it. A special mention and thank you to Jordan Fenn, Rob Howard and Michael Mouland, whose advice, counsel and intuitive grasp of the concepts underlying the manuscript were a great comfort and help throughout.

To all of the incredible chefs that contributed their wonderful recipes to the book, thank you for finding time in your unanimously frenzied schedules to participate in this project. Your recipes prove that healthy food can be as pleasing to our palettes as it is beneficial to our waistlines.

To doctors Bruce Topp and Susan Somerville, thank you for your unwavering support and encouragement and for allowing me to conduct the clinical research trial which offered proof of the diet's efficacy and acceptability amongst your patient population. I feel very lucky to have had the opportunity to work with you both.

Thank you to everyone who has reviewed and followed The Hershberg Diet. Your support, endorsements, testimonials, and stories of progress and success have meant the world to me.

I have been blessed with wonderful friends and family. To all of them, thank you from the bottom of my heart. You've shaped me, inspired me, nurtured me, motivated me, and put up with me—I love you all.

And to Tyler, my husband, partner, and best friend, this project would not have become what it is today without your help, advice, patience, love, and support. I am a better, stronger and smarter person because of you. Thank you for believing in me.

Trademark Information

Crystal Light soft drink is a registered trademark of Kraft Foods Holdings, Inc.

Danone is a registered trademark of Groupe Danone.

Fibre 1 is a registered tradmark of General Mills Inc.

Fudgsicle is a registered trademark of Good Humor-Breyers® Ice Cream Company.

Goldseal Tuna is a registered trademark of Canfisco.

I Can't Believe It's Not Butter is a registered trademark of Unilever United States, Inc.

Jell-O is a registered trademark of Kraft Foods Holdings, Inc., used under license.

McDonald's is a registered trademark of McDonald's Corporation.

Newman's Own is a registered trademark owned by No Limit, LLC.

PC Blue Menu Fibre First is a registered trademark of Loblaws, Inc.

Perrier is a registered trademark of Nestle waters North America.

Piller's is a registered trademark of Piller Sausages and Delicatessens Ltd.

Renee's is a registered trademark of Renee's Gourmet Foods Inc.

Silhouette is a registered trademark of Groupe Danone.

Splenda is a registered trademark of McNeil Nutritionals, a Division of McNeil-PPC, Inc.

Sugar Twin is a registered trademark of Alberto-Culver USA, Inc.